THE
NEW AGE
SECRET PLAN
FOR
WORLD
CONQUEST

Salem Kirban

AMG
PUBLISHERS

P.O. Box 22000 • 6815 Shallowford Rd. • Chattanooga, TN 37422

First AMG Publishers edition, revised 1992

ISBN: 0–89957–621–4

Printed in the United States of America.

Contents

How The
NEW AGE CONSPIRACY BEGAN!

The New Age Movement began when Nimrod built his Babylonian Tower "to reach the Heavens." The thin line of Satan's conspiracy continued through the Sumerians, Egyptians and the mystic cults of China and India. The Druids introduced secret societies and godless Israel originated the 5-pointed star.

PART ONE

1

NIMROD HAD A BETTER IDEA . . .

**AT LEAST . . .
THAT'S WHAT HE THOUGHT!**

**Are We
Becoming
Cafeteria
Christians?**

Nimrod thought he could build a better world by setting forth his own rules!

Sound familiar?

Here we are some 5000 or more years later and still we try to formulate our own "religion of convenience" that allows us to formulate our own theology. Even believers who once stood for the fundamentals of the faith have now transformed themselves into "cafeteria Christians" picking and choosing those doctrines that best conform to their lifestyles. And since they find that most Bible doctrine does not fit their "modern" way of living . . . they develop their own theology . . . the theology of the "liberated" Christian.

What they forget is that Nimrod [about **3000** B.C.] had the same idea. Actually, it wasn't even Nimrod's idea. **It was Satan's!** Lucifer [angel of Light] became Satan [prince of the Darkness] because of his ambitious pride. Beginning with Eve he planned **The Great Conspiracy!**

About 100 years after the Flood, the first empire was built under Nimrod. Nimrod wanted to build a city and a tower that would reach to heaven. This was the beginning of humanism and the New Age line of ambitious conspiracy.

**Made Only
For
Heavenly
Existence!**

What you must understand is that Satan's body was made for <u>heavenly</u> existence.

Unlike the Lord God, Satan **cannot** materialize his body to appear in earthly form. Instead he has to control and appropriate someone else's body!

Satan has a continuing unrelenting hatred towards God. He is engaged in a world–wide and age–long struggle against God. His goal is to defeat the divine plans of grace toward mankind and to seduce men to evil and their eventual ruin. Satan is known as the ". . . deceiver of the whole world." See Revelation 12:9.

THE THIN LINE OF CONSPIRACY

**Fallen Angels
Are
Satan's Army**

In Satan's original rebellion against God it is revealed that

> ". . . his tail [Satan's] swept away a third part
> of the stars of heaven . . ."

> (Revelation 12:4)

These fallen angels who became Satan's army have apparently retained much or all of the power, and all the wisdom that they had <u>before</u> the fall! They are now, as fallen angels, called **demons**!

Satan's first target in the great conspiracy was to enlist Adam and Eve into his vast army and destroy the plan of God. Since he could not materialize his body on earth . . . in tempting Eve . . . he used the body of a serpent! For this job he pulled out his favorite tool of trade . . . the tool of deception! It worked!

With that victory in hand he set out to further his gains and set his sights on **Nimrod!**

Nimrod . . . Founder of BABYLON!

Now Nimrod was Noah's great–grandson through Ham. He was the founder of Babylon. And here we have the origins of Antichrist and the False Prophet!

Babel was the beginning of his kingdom which gradually enlarged [Genesis 10:8–10]. Today it would be located in the country of Iraq.

About 100 years after the Flood, the first empire was built under Nimrod. Remember . . . at that time, the whole world spoke only **one** language [Genesis 11:1].

Doing It His Way!

But Nimrod and his associates had what they thought was a better idea! They said:

> *"Let us build us a <u>city</u> and a <u>tower</u>, whose top may reach up to heaven; and let us make us a name lest we be scattered abroad upon the face of the whole earth."*
>
> [Genesis 11:4]

Does this sound like modern TV evangelists who strive to build empires here on earth? Well, this was over 4000 years ago! And you will discover "there is nothing new under the sun!"

Nimrod wanted to build a <u>city</u>. This represented the **material** side of life . . . power and wealth. It will have its culmination in **Antichrist**.

Nimrod also wanted to build a tower. This represented the **religious** side of life. It will have its final fulfillment in the **False Prophet.**

God Brought Confusion To Their Plan

What happened to Nimrod's Tower of Babel? God brought judgment by confounding [mixing up] their language so they could not understand each other. That's why you have to study Spanish and French!

We have gone from a unified language in Genesis 3 to more than 3000 different languages today. And only 30 are spoken by more than 10 Million people!

Now there is a New Age conspiracy to reduce the present population of the earth [5 Billion] to only 1 Billion of which 500 Million will be Chinese!

More people speak Chinese today [1 Billion] than any other language . . . more than <u>double</u> the number of people that speak English!

In 1887, a Polish Jew, Ludwig Zamenhof, designed an artificial language with a 28–letter alphabet. He called it <u>Esperanto</u>, meaning "one who hopes."

Now We Suffer With Many Languages!

Since the 1600's over 700 artificial languages have been created in the hopes of having <u>one unified universal language</u>! So, if you grumbled because you had to study another language . . . <u>blame it on Nimrod</u>!

While God destroyed Babylon their sin left us with a legacy of a multiplicity of languages. And this has brought further confusion because it makes it difficult for people to communicate rapidly with people of other nations. This then becomes an excellent breeding ground for distrust and wars and rumors of wars.

Even English
Is Not
Uniform

Even the Americans and British have different words for the same thing. In the United States we call it an <u>apartment</u>. The British say it's a <u>flat</u>. We say it's an <u>automobile</u>. They say <u>motorcar</u>. We call it <u>gasoline</u>. They call it <u>petrol</u>.

The Tower of Babel, engineered by Satan through Nimrod, was an attempt by man to build a united world society from which God was to be excluded.

2

ENTER THE SENSUAL SUMERIANS

THEY BEGAN THE PROBLEMS
OF THE PERSIAN GULF

**Sumerians . . .
An Intelligent
People**

We can thank the Babylonians for "blessing" us with a multiplicity of languages! And if that wasn't enough punishment . . . along came a people called the **Sumerians**.

About 4000 B.C. the Sumerians migrated to the area called <u>Mesopotamia</u> from what is now known as Russia. No, Mesopotamia is not the name of a disease. The word means "the land between the Rivers." It is a land at the head of the Persian Gulf.

Now these people had above average intelligence. They knew how to write. And one didn't have to wait in endless lines at their post offices! Their system of wedge–shaped characters inscribed on clay tablets are man's earliest written records.

Believe it or not, they had developed not only a potter's wheel but also a wagon wheel! Men shaved and women had shoes of soft leather, heel–less and laced like our own. They even wore bracelets, anklets, finger rings and earrings!

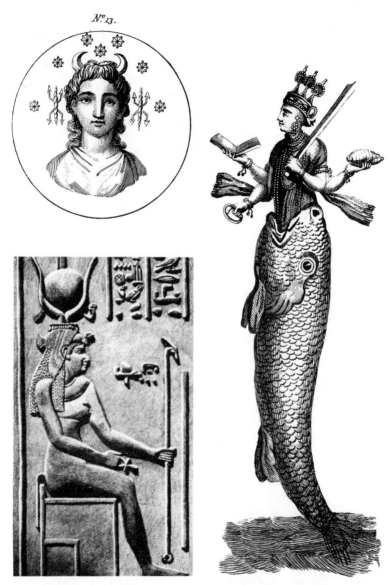

(Top left) Ashtaroth (Ishtar/Babylonian Mother of god). (Bottom left) Isis, goddess of nature in ancient Egypt. (Right) Dagon, Philistine and Phoenician God of agriculture.

**Revolving
Doors On
Huts!**

The government did not control the post office but they did control the weaving industry. And, look at this . . . the Sumerians [some 6000 years ago] had revolving doors on their huts! Gold and silver was the medium of exchange. And while they did not have freeways and busy turnpikes, one tablet bears a message complaining of:

". . . the city, where the tumult of man is."

They had contracts and courts but lawyers were not popular or tolerated. In fact, to keep people out of court . . . every case was first submitted to a public arbitrator!

**Pantheism . . .
"God is not
a person . . ."**

The Sumerian culture introduced <u>two</u> groups of gods which brought **pantheism** into existence.

> <u>Pantheism</u> is the doctrine that God is not a person, but that all forces are manifestations of God.

Pantheism advocates tolerance of the worship of <u>all</u> the gods of various cults.

The Sumerians worshiped, as an example,

Anum – the sky god and king of the gods

Utu –   the god of the sun

Innin – the lady of heaven later called Venus

Ishtar – the god of love and war

Women were attached to every temple. And every woman was obliged, once in her life, to sit in the temple of Venus and submit to immoral acts before she could return home. This was to be an offering to the god of love, Ishtar.

Scene shows worship of Bel, patron god of Babylon. The Lord
promised: "I will punish Bel in Babylon, and I will bring forth out of
his mouth that which he hath swallowed up; and the nations shall
not flow together any more unto him: yea, the wall of Babylon shall
fall" (Jeremiah 51:44).

Feminism Is Not New!

At the temple, prostitutes were in abundance. Women could engage in business independently of her husband. They had cosmetics, cuticle sticks and tweezers! And every bride kept her dowry!

In Sumeria, each city had its own gods. One Sumerian city mentioned in the Old Testament is the city of **Ur**. This city was the home of Terah and the birthplace of his son, Abram [who was to become Abraham]. Actually, the first Jew was a Gentile. And the first Hebrew was a heathen.

Terah served a host of Sumerian gods . . . as did his son, Abram. But God chose Abraham to become the father of a new spiritual race and inheritance.

About 2000 B.C. Abraham left Ur along with his father, Terah, and family for Haran in the land of Canaan. (See Genesis 11:31.) Ur was destroyed about 1950 B.C. and Sumeria fell to Hammurabi's Babylonian empire about 1728 B.C.

EVERY ANT IS A GOD [NO WONDER THERE'S WAR IN THE PERSIAN GULF!]

No Hope Of Immortality!

Venus was often pictured as a bisexual deity. Both the Babylonians and the Sumerians had no hope of immortality. Like the Greeks, they believed the dead went to a dark and shadowy realm within the bowels of the earth, and none of them saw the light again. Heaven was only for the gods.

**Ishtar . . .
Mother of Baal**

Ishtar, the god of love, was known as the Queen of Heaven. In the Old Testament she is called "Ashtoreth" which means in Hebrew, "shame." She was known as the mother of Baal.

You recall in Judges, chapters 2 and 6, when Gideon pulled down his father's altar of Baal and cut down the Ashtoreth symbol, that he did so by night because he was too afraid to do it by day.

It was this god of love [Ishtar or Astarte] who was associated with the moon, and often shown with the horns of the crescent moon. Temple attendants were eunuchs who wore white robes with pointed caps. [Does this remind you of the Ku Klux Klan?]

**Watching
Ants
For Guidance**

Horns have become the symbol of power, and horns, crescent moon, and pointed caps all are occult symbols which are still used today. Among the witchcraft practices in that day were the interpretation of dreams, astrology, the slaughtering of animals and examining their organs to determine future events.

Omens were even obtained by watching ants!

Activity was centered around the temples . . . and the wealth of the temples grew. **Marduk** became the high god . . . the god of the sun. The King was initiated by priests, swearing allegiance to the god **Bel** [the god of heaven and earth] as he carried the image of <u>Marduk</u> through the streets.

Little has changed today from some 4000 years ago. We still have men parading in white robes

**Worshiping
The Sun**

with pointed hats. Astrology is a multi–million dollar business. We still worship the sun. It was on Wednesday, May 3, 1978, that the United States paid homage to the sun. It was called Sun Day.

And the many gods of the Sumerians helped give birth to what we call today secular humanism . . . where we worship the creature instead of the creator. With the Babylonians, the Sumerians further advanced the program of Satan in the great conspiracy.

And while we may not watch ants to foretell the future . . . we don't even work as energetically as ants! But, of course, ants never did have their own union. Why didn't they think of it!

3

THE RISE OF SECRET SOCIETIES

IT BEGAN BY WORSHIPING OAK TREES!

Druids . . .
A Mystical
Occult
Society

Druids are mentioned by name in some 30 references by Greek and Roman writers between the 2nd century B.C. and the 4th century A.D.

Druids are members of a Celtic religious order of mystic priests who originated in ancient Britain, Ireland and France. The word Druid means

"the men of the oak trees."

About 1245 A.D. a gathering of Druids was held with representatives from many geographical regions and the objectives of the Order of Druids was agreed upon. A grove was founded in England which still exists today, Mount Hawmus Grove.

Druids, along with Rosicrucians and Freemasons are a mixture of mystical–occult societies which were influenced by the mystic Jacob Boehme (1575–1624).

Boehme made popular the theory that the Trinity was: (1) the sky, (2) the sun, and (3) the light. Boehme further believed that just as God is threefold, so man being created in the image God is threefold. Thus, Boehme developed the

**The
Three Birth
Theology**

<u>**THRICE BORN**</u> or <u>**THREE BIRTHS**</u> theology. It should be noted that several very prominent "Christians" claim to be "thrice born." The origin of such statements can only be attributed to witchcraft and the occult.

Boehme reasoned:

1. The "elemental birth" gave man his body.
2. The "astral birth" gives him his instincts and intelligence which he shares with other animals.
3. The "spiritual birth" gives man the "divine essence," the ingredient in him which is potentially God.

Now can you see the origin of the theory that New Agers adopt . . . "we are gods."

Boehme combined Christian mysticism and Cabbala. Cabbala is an occult numerical philosophy developed by Jewish Rabbis in the Middle Ages.

**Offered
Human
Sacrifices!**

The Druids picked up some of this philosophy and incorporated it into their mysticism. The secret teachings of the Druids were never written, but they were communicated orally to specially prepared candidates. Such practices continue in modern day witchcraft in the Council of 13 and in the Mason's Council of 33.

The Druids controlled all education in their day. To appease their gods, they offered human sacrifices of men condemned to death.

The Druids, as do witches today, believed in reincarnation. They believed in a purgatorial type of hell where they would be purged of their

The Druids were the teachers and priests of ancient Britain, Gaul, and Ireland. They considered the hours of noon and midnight sacred and performed their rites in the light of the full moon.

sins, afterward passing on to the happiness of unity with the gods.

Going Around More Than Once!

The Druids taught that all men would be saved, but that some must return to earth many times to learn the lessons of human life and to overcome the inherent evil of their own nature.

Before a candidate was entrusted with the secret doctrines of the Druids, he was bound with a vow of secrecy. These doctrines were revealed only in the depths of forests and in the darkness of caves.

The Druids celebrated a number of feast days. At dawn on the 25th day of December, the birth of the Sun God was celebrated. The Druids had a Madonna, or Virgin Mother, with a Child in her arms; and their Sun God was resurrected at the time of the year corresponding to that at which we celebrate Easter. It is amazing how Satan becomes the great imitator!

The Druids worshiped the sun, moon and stars. They also worshiped the serpent. The famous Stonehenge in Southwestern England is a Druid altar.

Initiates had to pass through three degrees of the Druid Mysteries. Few successfully passed them all.

They included burying the candidate in a coffin and sending him out to sea in an open boat. Those who reached the third degree became prominent British religious and political leaders. Druids came out of the Celtic culture. The Celts practiced human sacrifice. They sacrificed

Ritual
Drownings

adults as well as infants and had ritual drownings. The number <u>three</u> was sacred to the Celts. Such mysticism and occultism became part of the Druid tradition.

Druid priests exist today . . . and evidence indicates that ritual sacrifice is also still practiced today in some areas! And the thin line of Satan's continuing conspiracy goes on!

Druids . . . the men of the oak trees!

Remember that . . . the next time you pick up a toothpick! It might have come from a "holy" oak!

THE ARCH-DRUID IN HIS
CEREMONIAL ROBES.

KIS meant "Holy the God of the Septenary." "Septenary" means seven.

4

UNCOVERING A SECRET FROM ANCIENT ISRAEL

**RITUALS AND SYMBOLS
NEW AGERS USE TODAY**

**The Cabala . . .
A New
Theology**

About 120 A.D. <u>Rabbi Akiba</u> came up with what he thought was a better idea. He wanted to "improve" upon the Scriptures. So he wrote a book based upon a <u>mystical</u> interpretation of the Scriptures. It became known as the **Cabala** . . . an occult society.

Cabala is sometimes spelled <u>Cabbala</u> or <u>Qabbalah</u>. The Hebrew word is <u>Kabbalah</u>. This means "receiving" or "that which is received."

Many believe this secret lore began with the group called the **Essenes**. The Essenes flourished from 2 B.C. to 135 A.D. They were mostly unmarried and filled their ranks by newcomers joining them and by adopting other people's children. They were required to take secret oaths. They had their own purification rites. The name "Essenes" supposedly is derived from an ancient Syrian word meaning "physician." The Essenes had three degrees of progression members had to go through.

Cabalists had a preoccupation with letters and names of God, as containers of secret knowledge. Circular symbol at left, hung around the neck before sunrise on a Sunday was supposed to make the wearer invisible. Triangular symbol at right shows the Hebrew letter W, used to signify the trinity sapphires *(Sephiroth).*

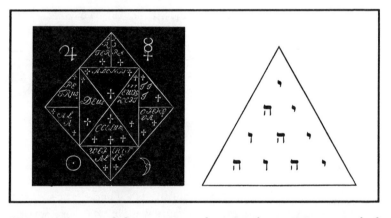

Diagram square at left was supposed to give the magician control of all evil spirits. The Tetragrammaton (meaning 4 letters) were the four consonants of the ancient Hebrew name for God. By arranging the four letters of the *"Great Name of God,"* Cabalists believed the 72 powers of the *"Great Name of God"* were manifested.

Salvation Through Secret Knowledge

Cabala teachings came from a background of mysticism including that of the **Gnostics**. The Gnostics believed that people could be saved through secret knowledge.

Gnostics believed that salvation depended solely upon the knowledge of one's "spiritual" nature.

This gave them a license to live a life of sin. (Does it remind you of "cafeteria Christians" today who want the best of both worlds?)

Some Gnostic leaders urged their followers to sin. They taught that promiscuity was God's law and that since they were "pearls," they could not be stained by any external mud.

Many believed that humans were originally unisex . . . that the creation of woman was the source of evil. They taught that Jesus was merely a man.

Cabala theology had Gnostic[1] influence. They believed that even every stone, every plant cries out for salvation. This strange theology penetrated much of Europe and by the 17th century it was closely associated with magic.

Now it has grown to include diverse kinds of occult practice and divination (fortune telling). The 22 major cards of the Tarot pack are connected with the 22 Paths used by those who practiced Cabala. Tarot cards are "fortune telling" cards. The Cabala promoted a strange theology

---

[1]**Gnostic** means "one who knows." **Agnostic** means "one who doesn't know." An agnostic believes that the human mind cannot know whether there is a God.

which now is even evident in the Catholic church.

A Hidden Doctrine

The Cabala taught that within God's Word existed a hidden doctrine which was the key to the Scriptures [sounds like Mary Baker Eddy].

This secret doctrine is symbolized by the crossed keys upon the papal crest. The theories of Cabala are now intertwined with the doctrines of magic, of Rosicrucianism and Freemasonry.

The Cabala promoted the use of so–called magic symbols. They used the Tetragrammaton [meaning 4 letters] as a sort of magic talisman. The four letters were the four consonants of the ancient Hebrew name for God. Generally spelled **JHVH** or **YHWH,** the name of God was considered too sacred to be spoken in utterance.

In the 16th century, John Reuchlin (a "Christian" Cabalist) maintained that the name of Jesus (the **Penta**grammaton) exceeds the **Tetra**grammaton in power by adding the letter **S** to it. Thus **JHVH** becomes **JHSVH.** Thus, since Penta means **5** (the five letters for Jesus . . . **JHSVH**), the star with its five points became to the cultists a weapon of power in magic.

> A pentagram (5 pointed star) with **one** of its points projecting upwards was to them a symbol of divine spirit.
>
> A reversed pentagram with **two** points projecting upwards represents a symbol of evil and suggests the horns of the Devil.

Modern magicians still use the pentagram. In gnostic schools it is called the blazing star and denotes the sign of intellectual omnipotence. <u>The Order of the Golden Dawn</u> (formed by 3 members of the Rosicrucian Society in England) use the Pentagram.

The Penalty of Serving Other Gods!

Most Jews today do not follow the Cabala philosophies. But with the increase of witchcraft and secret societies, many of its doctrines are being promoted today.

God had long reminded the people of Israel that if they did not follow Him and would:

> . . . go and serve other gods, and worship them;
> Then will I pluck them up by the roots out of
> my land which I have given them . . .
>
> (2 Chronicles 7:19,20)

Those that saw this occurring in Israel would ask why the Lord scattered this nation and allowed them to suffer hardships. God's answer was:

> Because they forsook the Lord of their fathers,
> which brought them out of the land of Egypt,
> and laid hold on other gods . . . and worshiped
> them, and served them, therefore hath He
> brought all this evil upon them.
>
> (2 Chronicles 7:22)

This is not to imply that all the evil cults of today had their origin from Hebrews of yesterday. This is simply not true!

While many of the people of Israel did reject God many times throughout Scripture and worship evil gods, the Gentiles were even more guilty in their pursuit of evil.

5

YIN and YANG

PLUS OTHER CULTS OF CONFUSION

**3000 Chinese
Jump
To Death
In
Lake of Wine!**

The New Age movement . . . not willing to accept the triune living God . . . seek their salvation through far eastern cults created by the
Chinese and the religious sects of India.

To New Agers these eastern religions hold an
aura of mystery and antiquity to them. And
while they may not realize it . . . they are set-
tling for the chaff . . . which at the Judgment,
will be blown away!

China gave birth to humanistic philosophies.
Humanism is an atheistic philosophy which
holds that man is capable of self–fulfillment
without recourse to God.

Chinese Emperor Chieh [1818–1766 B.C.] brought
the first dynasty of China to a close. He was an
atheist. He amused himself and his wife by com-
pelling 3000 Chinese to jump to their death in
a lake of wine! Emperor Chou Hsin, the inven-
tor of chopsticks, ordered a man's chest cut open
so he could see if his heart had seven chambers.
His wife was equally as cruel.

It was China that spawned the humanistic, meta-
physical book *I–Ching,* or "Book of Changes."

Their theory was that there was a <u>single</u> cosmic
cell containing <u>ether</u> [Ch'i] which was made to

Yin & Yang . . .
Female
And
Male

pulsate by a creative force known as <u>Tao</u>.

Tension set up by this activity eventually split the cell into opposite and complimentary halves, so they believed. Thus twin <u>ethers</u> which encompassed the universe were called by them,

Yin and **Yang**

Yin / is of the earth, dark, female

Yang / is of heaven, bright, male

The Chinese believe that the continuous operation of <u>Tao</u> (which they suppose to be a natural law), causes <u>Yin</u> and <u>Yang</u> to alternate . . . and by this process . . . <u>five</u> "elements" are produced: water, fire, wood, metal and earth. Their theory is that this evolves the creation process.

The Chinese used *I–Ching* (The Book of Changes) as a manual for telling the future. And it is widely used today in New Age circles.

Most of China encompasses three basic religions: Confucianism, Buddhism and Taoism.

Yin and Yang
In Chinese philosophy, two great opposite principles or forces, on whose interplay everything in the universe depends; Yang is male, light and positive, Yin is female, dark and negative, and all phenomena can be classified in terms of them; in Taoism, the Tao is the principle which unites and transcends the opposites.

**Demons and Spirits
Theology**

Confucius [Kung Fu–tze/550–480 B.C.]

Confucius was an agnostic. Man had no special destiny. Confucius did not believe in
eternal life.

Buddha [Gotama/576–483 B.C.]

Gotama became known as Buddha and was
called "the enlightened one." Buddhists believe in many demons and spirits. They deny
there is personal world–creator. They deny
that there is a personal soul. Instead Buddhists
believe that there is personal continuity from
life to life through many rebirths . . . reincarnation. This is a New Age philosophy.

New Agers seek a perfect One World through
"enlightenment." To achieve "enlightenment" one must get off the endless wheel of
birth, death, rebirth . . . and again, birth,
death, rebirth, etc. Getting away from this
cycle was called reaching **Nirvana.**

Nirvana is described by New Agers as the
state of perfect blessedness achieved by the
extinction of individual existence.

To reach Nirvana one is told that he must
follow the **Holy Eightfold Path:** (1) right views,
(2) right intention, (3) right speech (4) right
action, (5) right livelihood, (6) right effort,
(7) right mindfulness and (8) right concen-
tration. This last "Path" is where meditation
comes in.

Taoism [Lao Tze/604 B.C.–517 B.C.]

Tao means "course" or "way." Its secret society teachings and witchcraft are occult and

**Promoting
Pseudo–science**

confusing. It began in China. Although it claims to show the way . . . it points to no particular way. It has since been adopted by many New Age groups. Credited to Taoists are:

Astrology

a pseudo–science which claims to foretell the future by studying the supposed influence of the relative positions of the moon, sun and stars on human affairs.

Acupuncture

a system of healing where needles are inserted into the skin to a depth of about a tenth of an inch. Acupuncture is based on the <u>Yin and Yang</u> philosophy.

**The Worship
Of Many Gods**

Hinduism assimilated much of the Buddhist cult religion. Hinduism has no founder. "<u>Hindu</u>" is a Persian word that simply means "<u>Indian</u>." The Hindus worship many gods, including **Shiva** and its female counterpart, **Shakti.**

From this emerged one of the most satanic cults of the East, **Tantrism**. <u>Tantrism</u> dwells on sexual excessiveness, advocating complete sexual freedom. Sexual organs are even worshiped as a god. It is this strange cult that originated **Yoga** [a yoke]. <u>Yoga</u> attempts to free the soul from all bodily attachment in an attempt to attain supreme enlightenment and salvation in one life <u>by atoning</u> in one existence for all sins of the soul's <u>past</u> lives or incarnations.

Yoga originates in <u>Tantrism</u>. Great emphasis is laid on respiratory exercises and the control of

Faithfulness through marriage and in marriage brings Christian growth and fruitfulness. However, humanism has crept into the Church compromising standards.

Tantrists were among the first to introduce sexual "freedom." And Satan will continue in his fight to compromise the effectiveness of the Christian.

what normally are autonomic functions. Autonomic functions are those body functions which are not normally controlled by the conscious mind, such as breathing, body temperatures, pulse rate.

Seven Segments Of Body Energy

Tantrists divide the body into 7 segments with energies that pass from the tail–bone up to the skull. They see the tail–bone being guarded by a tiny snake. The goal of the Tantrists is to awaken the snake so it begins its upward climb to the skull. If they can achieve this they believe their receive the ultimate sensual bliss.

Philosophically, their goal is to go against the established order of things. They believe "Actions that cause a man to burn in hell, are those by which the yogi attains beatitude." They also state that "Perfection is gained by satisfying all one's desires."

The Tantrists believe the act of sex can lead to salvation. One rite commonly celebrated is known as "circle worship." Male and female participants sit next to each other on the floor. In the middle of the circle sit another couple, representing **Shakti** and **Shiva.** Shakti represents the female and Shiva the male god. Then all the members partake of the ceremonial meal consisting of wine, meat, fish and bread. After this, through a system of random selection this banquet is followed by a rite of sexual intercourse.

Tantrists believe in the idealization of self. Their basic theme is: "What you desire, that do, for this gratifies the goddess **Shakti**." We can see how this satanic theology which started centuries ago is now having its harvest in the humanism of today.

The Theology Of Being Your Own Master!

Yoga, which is even taught in many schools and businesses in the United States . . . evolved from these curious cults of India.

It is form of humanism, which says: "I am the master of my ship."

Its advocates have prescribed it for anything from getting rid of migraine headaches to getting rich. There are many yoga positions . . . the most popular one being the cross–legged "Lotus" position.

Another is standing on your head, controlling your breathing and reciting repetitious phrases called mantras.

Standing on your head makes about as much sense as the other forms of Indian mysticism. The only advantage of standing on your head is that you can see the world **UPSIDE DOWN!**

6

ISLAM . . . A PARADOX OF CONFUSION

IT'S LIKE TRYING TO UNTANGLE A SEA OF BUBBLEGUM

Islam . . .
A Growing
Threat!

Paradox comes from the Greek.

"Para" means "contrary to."

"Dox" means "expectation."

Thus a paradox is something that is contrary to expectation! And Islam in the midst of today's Iran/Iraq/Middle East turmoil certainly fits this definition! For if they were true advocates of Islam . . . there would be peace in the Middle East.

Mohammed, founder of Islam, [in writings called the Hadith], said:

The best Islam is that you feed the hungry, spread peace among friends and strangers all over the world.

Today, Iran's actions are a far cry from peace.

Mohammed was born in Mecca [Saudi Arabia] about 570 A.D. Within 100 years of Mohammed's birth, these nomads would conquer half of Asia, all of Persia [Iran] and most of North Africa. These people were called Arabs. Arab means arid.

ISLAM

Followers: approx. 800 000 000

Countries:

Afghanistan
Algeria
Bahrain
Bangladesh
Benin
Egypt
Federation of Arabian Emirates (Abu
  Dhabi, Dubai, Ajman, Sharjah, Ras el
  Khaimah, Fujairah, Umm al Qaiwain
Indonesia
Iraq
Iran
Jordan
Qatar
Kuwait
Libya

Morocco
Mauritania
Niger
Oman
Pakistan
Saudi Arabia
Senegal
Somalia
Sudan
Syria
Tunisia
Turkey
Yemen (Arab Republic) = Arab-
    Islamic Republic
Yemen (People's Republic)
    = South Yemen

Moslems saying their prayers as prescribed by the Koran.

**The Perils
Of Being A
Woman!**

Although Bedouin women were of incomparable beauty . . . they were oppressed in those days and considered mere personal property [chattel]. When a girl was born into a family, the father could bury her at birth, if he so willed. At age 7 she was sold off to any youth of the clan for marriage . . . at a price! Her husband demanded of her many children. He often had many wives and he could dismiss her at any time.

This was the climate in which Mohammed was born. His new religion, Islam, only slightly improved the lot of women. Mohammed had 10 wives; other Muslims were permitted 4.

**Worshiping
A Stone**

In those days the Arabs worshiped a stone in Mecca. It was called **Kaaba.** The Kaaba was rebuilt about 10 times. They believed the first Kaaba was erected by angels from heaven; the second by Adam; the third by his son Seth; the fourth by Abraham and his son Ishmael by Hagar. The eighth was built in Mohammed's lifetime in 605 A.D.

It was at this time that the Kaaba contained several statues representing gods. One was called **Allah** [the "up one"] a tribal god. He was considered the Lord of the Soil. At age 40, Mohammed went to a cave near Mecca and claimed that the angel Gabriel appeared to him and said: "O Mohammed! thou art the messenger of Allah, and I am Gabriel." That was 610 B.C. From then on, Mohammed announced himself as the prophet of Allah. His first convert was his wife.

The Koran asserts that man is superior to woman: *"Men are superior to women on account of the qualities with which God has gifted the one above the other. . . ."*

The compulsory wearing of the veil is another rule outlined in the Koran. The veil developed into a complete costume covering the entire body, completely concealing the woman's features. Only the hands and feet showed. Muslim women have been suppressed in many ways particularly in the extreme sects.

**Muslims
Adopted
Several
Jewish Rites**

In the first days, the Muslims adopted several of the Jewish rites. They prayed facing Jerusalem, and Jewish fasts were observed. But when relations with the Jews became tense, Muslims were told to face Mecca when they prayed.

Mohammed would not stand for opposition. In one battle captured Jews were given the choice of choosing Islam or death. They were slain and buried in the market place of Medina. Their women and children were sold into slavery.

Although Mohammed had 10 wives and 2 concubines . . . all his wives, except his first, were barren. He gave considerable time to his personal appearance. He perfumed his body, painted his eyes and dyed his hair. Mohammed died in 632 A.D.

Mohammed taught that he was no more than one of a line of prophets; but his message was God's final word. Thus a new religion was founded called **ISLAM**. Islam is a word which indicates "submission to God." One who submits is called a **Moslem**.

MOHAMMED'S THEOLOGY OF HEAVEN

**Poor
Reach Heaven
500 Years
Before The Rich!**

Much of Mohammed's writings in the Koran tend to run parallel with Bible prophecy. He speaks of resurrections, a falling away in the last days, trumpet blasts and judgments.

In Mohammed's heaven, those who die for Allah's cause will reach it, along with the poor, 500 years before the rich. They will recline on

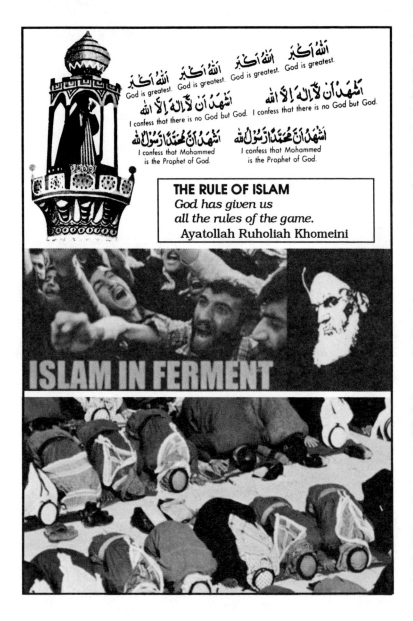

اللهُ أَكْبَر
God is greatest.
اللهُ أَكْبَر
God is greatest.
اللهُ أَكْبَر
God is greatest.
اللهُ أَكْبَر
God is greatest.
اللهُ أَكْبَر
God is greatest.

أَشْهَدُ أَنْ لَا إِلَهَ إِلَّا الله
I confess that there is no God but God.
أَشْهَدُ أَنْ لَا إِلَهَ إِلَّا الله
I confess that there is no God but God.
أَشْهَدُ أَنْ لَا إِلَهَ إِلَّا الله
I confess that there is no God but God.

أَشْهَدُ أَنَّ مُحَمَّدًا رَسُولُ الله
I confess that Mohammed
is the Prophet of God.
أَشْهَدُ أَنَّ مُحَمَّدًا رَسُولُ الله
I confess that Mohammed
is the Prophet of God.

THE RULE OF ISLAM
God has given us
all the rules of the game.
Ayatollah Ruholiah Khomeini

ISLAM IN FERMENT

In Islamic countries, Christians are opposed, prohibited or suppressed. Muslims who accept Christ face separation from their families and are often threatened or even killed by relatives!

couches and be served by handsome youths. They will drink wine from silver goblets and not get drunk. Many very young men in Iran and Iraq willingly sacrifice their lives on the battlefield because the Koran promises them a hasty flight to heaven where unusual benefits abound.

The Banquet Males Want To Attend!

One part of the Koran promises each male in heaven the following:

> By the mercy of Allah, there will be no speeches at these heavenly banquets; instead there will be virgins . . . with swelling bosoms but modest gaze. . . .
>
> Each blessed male will have 72 of these for his reward, and neither age nor weariness nor death shall mar the loveliness of these maidens, or their comrades' bliss.

> (lxxviii, 35; xliv, Koran)

Mohammed did not hold women in high esteem. The Koran speaks of women as man's supreme calamity, and suspects that most of them will go to hell. The Koran goes on to say that the wife should recognize the superior intelligence and therefore superior authority of the male [iv, 34]. Mohammed did admonish his followers to "Consort in the world kindly with Christians" [xxxl, 15].

ISLAM DIVIDES WORLD INTO TWO PARTS

In the religion of Islam, the world is divided into two parts:

1. The sphere of Islam
2. The sphere of war

The Theology
Of
Holy Wars

Islamic theology states that holy wars [jihad] are to be fought in the non–Islamic world so as to convert the pagans or to force the "people of the Book" [the Jews and Christians], to obligate themselves to pay a head–tax. They believe God created the earth in **two** days. They believe that Allah created the first man, Adam.

They say that beneath the earth are <u>six</u> hells.

They believe in angels and call them <u>**jinn**</u>. This is where we get our word **"<u>genie</u>."** They say angels were created from fire . . . thus the smoke . . . which accompanies the appearance of a "genie."

Moslems believe that Allah has sent 123,000 prophets to mankind, including Jesus.

Two of the major Muslim sects are:

1. **Sunnis**
   Five out of six of all Muslims in today's world are called Sunnis. They are the orthodox within Islam.

2. **Shiite**
   Mostly in Iran and Iraq . . . they believe that the "leader" is of paramount importance. This is the group from which the Ayatollah Khomeini emerged. The word "Ayatollah" means "Reflection of Allah."

Today Islam is sweeping the world! It has flooded Great Britain and is making inroads into the United States. Many Moslems are among the richest people in the world. A large proportion of the world's known reserves of oil is in Moslem territory. They control large blocks of wealth. They own many industries and control many banks in the United States. And New Age bankers have a plan to manipulate them to achieve their own One World goals. They want to control Moslem wealth.

Oddly enough, Mohammed taught that the rich will reach heaven 500 years **later** than the poor. Yet this does not seem to quench the Moslem zeal for gaining wealth in today's world.

7

THE SUBTLE SEDUCTION OF HUMANISM

THE THEOLOGY THAT DEIFIES MAN AND DETHRONES GOD

The Thin Line Of Conspiracy

From Lucifer's fall, to the tower of Babylon, the sensual Sumerians, the degenerate Druids, the rebellious people of Israel, the Chinese and Indian cults of confusion, the paradox of Islam . . . Satan's thin line of conspiracy is centered on one major theme . . . **humanism!**

It is this tool [humanism] above all others, that Satan uses with great skill hoping to achieve dominion over the entire world! Humanism is a deadly philosophy . . . a philosophy that is often used by Satan to deaden the effectiveness of Christian witness.

Humanism is a system of thought or action that holds that man is capable of self–fulfillment, peace on earth, and right ethical conduct <u>without</u> recourse to God.

Humanism, therefore, is the religion which deifies man and dethrones God!

Humanism has many facets. We see it evident as man attempts to control all of human life.

**Their
Sinister
Agenda!**

The acceptance of abortion . . . ending an unborn life . . . is a victory for the humanists. By the year 2000 the amount of the U.S. federal budget spent on those over the age of sixty–five will surpass $200 Billion Dollars a year. The prospect of this economic outlay has encouraged many humanists to favor the practice of euthanasia.

The word <u>euthanasia</u> is a compound of two words:

| <u>eu</u> | well |
| <u>thanatos</u> | death |

Thus the humanists would have everyone believe that <u>euthanasia</u> is a "painless, happy death." It is already practiced in a limited way in the United States. And in the Scandinavian countries it is performed by physicians. Thus, slowly, by gradualism, we are seeing the humanists take control even of life itself. No doubt, one day, they will duplicate Hitler's "Happy Farms" for the "over 65" set . . . designed to "free" them from this world . . . through euthanasia.

It is easy to see that within the near future euthanasia will be practiced freely in nursing homes or on those who ". . . have lived out their usefulness to society."

DESIGNER BABIES

But the humanists are not stopping there. Now, extensive studies are going on in what is called "genetic engineering."

The Society for the Right to Die and The Euthanasia Educational Council

Announce the adoption of the Tokyo Declaration at the First International Euthanasia* Conference

東京宣言一九七六年八月

In recent years, we have become aware of the increasing concern of the individual over his right to die with dignity, or euthanasia. We believe in the rights and freedom of all men. This brings us to affirm this right to die with dignity, which means in peace and without suffering.

Death is unavoidable. But we believe that the manner of dying should be left to the decision of the individual, assuming such demands do not result in harm to society other than the sadness associated with death.

The Declaration of a person's wishes, or the "Living Will," should be respected by all concerned as an expression of intrinsic human rights. Therefore, at least for the present, we request that this Declaration, or the "Living Will," be made legally effective, and pursuant to this, efforts toward its legalization should be made.

Through the Tokyo International Conference on Euthanasia, or Death with Dignity, the national movements of each country can achieve international cooperation, as well as solidarity. Let us promise ourselves to strive to achieve the above objectives, through the establishment of a liaison center whose purpose will be an exchange of information, as well as the convening of periodically held international conferences.

Tokyo Declaration of August, 1976

Australia Voluntary Euthanasia Society

by _____
Thomas I. Parramore

Japan Euthanasia Society

by _____
Tenrei Ota

Netherlands Voluntary Euthanasia Society

by _____
Nelly Folpmers

United Kingdom Voluntary Euthanasia Society

by _____
Charles R. Sweetingham

United States Society for the Right to Die

by _____
Sidney D. Rosoff

Euthanasia Educational Council

by _____
C. Dickerman Williams

*Euthanasia: eu — good   thanatos — death

**Are We Creating
A Monster?**

Genetic engineering is an attempt to control the type of individual that will be born by manipulating the genes.

Test tube babies are now a way of life. Now you can go to a sperm bank and tell them the type of child you would like to conceive! You can specify color of hair, color of eyes, short or tall height, IQ, passive or aggressive personality, and the potential of becoming career–oriented! Your desires are run through a computer which aligns your specifications with available sperm tubes in the bank. When a match is found, the wife is implanted with the sperm and conception occurs.

HUMANISTS WORSHIP THE CREATURE

**Worshiping
The Creature
Rather Than
The Creator**

Humanism is a doctrine which centers solely on human interests and values. True humanists do not believe in God nor do they believe in salvation through Jesus Christ nor the existence of a Heaven or Hell. Humanists worship the creature rather than the Creator!

Humanism's energies center on material values. In fact, we are seeing much of this satanic theology creep into our churches and religious television.

The humanist sees "sin" as primarily man's maladjustment to man. To the Christian, sin is disobedience to God's revealed will.

How many ministries and religious television programs have you seen that place emphasis

Do you want your child to be taught that Christ did not rise bodily, that Christ is not coming again? Do you want your child to be taught that sin is old-fashioned thinking and immorality is acceptable in today's world? That's the path Humanism is taking your children!

on buildings, the power of positive thinking, and building a better self–image . . . exclusive of preaching on man's sin and his need of a Saviour! These attitudes reflect humanist thinking which seek to capitalize on man's desire for success and wealth and a utopia here and now! They subtly seduce unsuspecting Christians into their camp and rob them of their tithes and offerings which should have gone to worthwhile ministries and missions who faithfully serve the Lord.

Humanism's Five Beliefs

Humanism, an effective arm of the New Age Movement, boasts of five basic beliefs in their doctrine:

1. The Irrelevance of Deity
Man's cooperative efforts towards social well–being are of prime importance. God has nothing to do with man's progress.

2. The Supremacy of "Human Reason"
Man alone can think out the answers to the great questions that confront mankind.

3. The Inevitability of Progress
Evolution is the answer to man's salvation. The State is the guardian angel that will control the environment and look after the best interests of man. [This leads, of course, to dictatorship]

4. Science, The Guide to Progress
Science itself will be the ultimate provider for mankind. Science will come up with genetic answers to provide a more uniform, manageable population.

5. The Self–Sufficiency of Man

Man is inherently good and is in no need of salvation. Man is autonomous [can function independently] without help from God.

Many people confuse the words <u>humane</u>, <u>humanities</u>, or <u>humanitarian</u> with the doctrine of **humanism.**

<u>Humane</u> is a quality marked by compassion.

<u>Humanitarianism</u> is simply an individual who promotes human welfare and social reform.

A **<u>Humanist</u>, however, is anti–God and believes** the theology that Man is the Captain of his Ship.

ORIGIN OF HUMANISM

Humanists and Communists Follow Same Path

Humanism basically began in Renaissance Italy [about 1400 A.D.] when the principal writers of the Middle Ages made a cult of man's human powers. They revived the works of Plato, Homer, Horace and Cicero and also Dante's *Divine Comedy* which he wrote in 1300 A.D.

The Communists of the Soviet Union (now C.I.S.) are actually today's example of the ultimate secular humanist! [And Humanists are allies of the New Age movement.] Look at these comparisons between Humanists and Communists:

Both deny the supernatural.

Both deny Divine revelation.

Both promote world government.

Both seek to destroy Christianity.

Both seek to control the educational system.

We Are Now Reaping A Wild Harvest!

Humanists have gained control of the educational system in the United States. And we are seeing now what a wild harvest it is reaping!

Humanism is a sinister, subtle seduction that comes in the back door while you are at the front door keeping alert for the enemy! Don't get caught off guard. Satan has many tricks up his sleeve! Humanism is one of his most effective.

The
NEW AGE CONSPIRACY EXPOSED!

How Adam Weishaupt founded a secret order he called the Illuminati! His 7-point Master Plan to create a World Government! Discover how this plan gave birth to a conspiracy of International Bankers . . . determined to control world markets. Reveals how they started World Wars 1 and 2 with goals for a One World system!

PART TWO

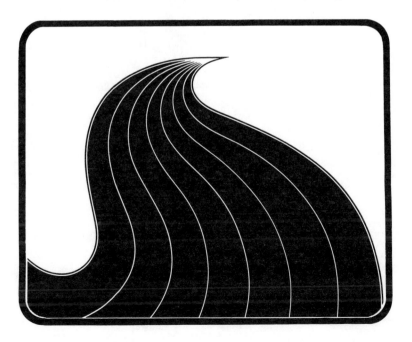

8

WITCHES DON'T RIDE ON BROOMS!

BUT . . . THEY MAY ENJOY FAST CARS!

Claiming To Have Supernatural Power

Witches today refer to their religion as **"Wicca."**

When most people think of witches, they may reflect on the Wizard of Oz and the good witch and the bad witch. This is a fairy tale and not true to life. But there is no such thing as a "good" witch!

A witch is a woman who claims to have supernatural power by a compact with the devil or evil spirits. Another name is <u>sorceress</u>.

In Deuteronomy 18:9–14 we learn that witchcraft was forbidden in Israel. Witches in Bible days used occult formulas surrounded with mystic mutterings or "magic" words. They still do today!

It is interesting to note that the word translated "witchcraft" in Galatians 5:20, "pharmakeia," literally denotes the act of administering <u>drugs</u> and giving of magical potions!

Witchcraft was practiced by Jezebel:

> . . . when Joram saw Jehu, he said, Is it peace, Jehu?
>
> And he answered, What peace, as long as the

> *harlotries of thy mother, Jezebel, and her witch-crafts are so many?*
>
> [2 Kings 9:22]

WITCHCRAFT CONDEMNED BY GOD

**Condemned
In
Scripture**

Witchcraft was condemned by the prophets, and through Micah, God revealed to Israel that in the future Millennium of 1000 years . . .

> *I will cut off witchcrafts . . . thou shalt have no more soothsayers [fortune tellers] Thy graven images also will I cut off. . . .*
>
> [Micah 5:12,13]

In 2 Chronicles 33:6, we find that witchcraft was practiced by Manasseh and abolished during the reign of Josiah [2 Kings 23:24].

Witchcraft, among other things, is the work of the flesh [Galatians 5:20].

HOW WITCHCRAFT BEGAN

**Origins
In
Babylon**

Witchcraft . . . as with other New Age conspiracies . . . had its origin in Babylon! In Babylon there were 53 temples of the great gods, 55 shrines dedicated to Marduk [the chief god of the sun] plus hundreds of other shrines. There were 80 altars alone to Ishtar [the goddess of love and fertility]. The Babylonians, remembered for their Tower of Babel, practiced fortune telling and astrology.

Ancient sorcerers were often necromancers. **Necromancy** is the practice of claiming to be able to foretell the future by alleged communication with the dead.

Popularized In The Middle Ages

Witchcraft, as we know it today, became again popular in the 13th century AD. From the 1200's to well into the 18th century, church and state joined hands to torture and burn witches. Near the end of the 17th century, 55 persons suffered by torture and 20 were put to death in Salem, Massachusetts.

In medieval times a witch was considered to be one who had sold her soul to Satan in exchange for magical powers. Medieval illustrations generally picture the witch as naked and flying through the air on broom handles, generally leaving the house through the chimney.

FALSE TIE WITH SOLOMON

Satan Pictured As a Goat

In their superstitions, witches met before the throne of Satan who was a goat. One witch would present a child to the demon. Novices were given a black book in exchange for the Gospels which they were renouncing. They were then stripped of their clothes to imitate the nudity of Adam and Eve. It is said that in France alone, under the reign of Charles IX, there were over 100,000 witches.

Much of the black book of sorcery attempts to tie in Solomon with its rites. (It is interesting that both Islam and Freemasonry also tie in with Solomon.) In one French book, called *La Clavicule de Salomon,* on page thirty is introduced the

Failure to follow the Lord always ends in tragedy. "There is a way which seemeth right unto a man but the end thereof are the ways of death" (Proverbs 14:12). Judas found this out. When Saul, faced with a superior enemy and the discouragement of his own army, acted on his own . . . it led to Endor. This illustration shows Samuel appearing, having been called by the witch of Endor (now called a medium). Saul had previously sinned in deliberate disobedience when he spared Agag and the best of the cattle God had told him to destroy. See 1 Samuel 15:9.

famous "magic circle." Supposedly, anyone who enters into communication with demons must be enclosed in this circle. The circle is nine feet in diameter and has 5–pointed stars.

SEX CHARMS CREATED

Arousing Sexual Love

In medieval days, professional witches were called upon to prepare **philters,** a potion or charm thought to arouse sexual love or produce a death–spell. It was here that the <u>divining rod</u> had its origin! The divining rod is a forked branch or stick alleged to reveal hidden water or minerals by dipping forward. The words **dowsing** or **witching** are used interchangeably with **divining**.

In European folklore, the two annual occasions when witches meet are April 30th and October 31st [Hallowe'en]. Practitioners of witchcraft today organize into **covens**. A coven is a group of six male and six female witches with a high priest or priestess. They meet monthly at the time of the full moon. They also meet at eight other occasions they call **sabbats** [the witches' sabbath].

BLACK MAGIC

Witchcraft has been divided by some into **black** magic and **white** magic. Those who practice <u>black</u> magic usually declare openly they are serving the devil. They are Satan worshipers.

Missionaries on the field often come into contact with the evidence of this cult. In Europe, much of black magic witchcraft comes from the <u>Sixth</u> and <u>Seventh Books of Moses</u>, false magic-type books, which they allege were written by Moses. To possess these is supposedly to possess the power of Lucifer!

WHITE MAGIC

A Warping Of Biblical Values

Those who practice **white** magic declare that they invoke the name of God, not Satan, and they use Biblical phrases. To practice white magic, however, is to use the name of God and Christ in a manner that violates the Lord's will!

Dr. Merrill F. Unger sums up the distinction between religious white magic and Biblical faith and prayer as follows:

> *In biblical faith, trust is placed solely in the Lord Jesus,*
>
> *In white magic, it is deflected to someone else [the human agent] or to something else [one's own faith]*
>
> *In biblical prayer of faith the praying person subjects himself to the will of God.*
>
> *In white magic the help of God is demanded under the assumption that exercising such power is in accordance with God's will.*
>
> *In white magic the Christian's markings are mere decorations that camouflage the magical means for knowledge and power.*
>
> [Merril F. Unger
> *Demons in the World Today*, p. 86]

ORIGIN OF WICCA

**The Witch
Queen Of
Heaven**

Modern witches refer to their religion as **"<u>Wicca</u>"** the feminine form of an Old English word meaning <u>witch</u>. In Wicca, there are both male and female members but the cult is mainly governed by the high priestess. She is referred to as the Queen of Heaven and her symbols are the moon and stars. Wicca is basically a fertility cult. Witch theology attempts to point out that Christ, with his 12 disciples had an ideal coven with the Virgin Mary as "high priestess."

GARTER, BADGE OF OFFICE

**The Garter
A Symbol**

In modern witchcraft the garter has always been the high priestess badge of office. Edward III [1327–1377] openly displayed the garter and acknowledged that he was a witch. He supposedly founded the "double coven" of the Order of the Garter in the witches' honor.

A girdle consisting of three cords and a black-handled knife is common to all members of a coven.

In a coven ceremony, in the center of their circle stands a small altar, upon which is placed the <u>Book of Shadows</u>, a copy of the liturgy of Wicca, plus containers for salt and water, a censer, a scourge, a wand, a pentacle [5–pointed star] and a chalice.

CEREMONY IN THE NUDE

**Nudity
And
Ceremonial
Whipping**

The naked witches stand just inside the circle with the high priestess at the center, kneeling at the altar. She mixes the salt with the water in a small bowl and then sprinkles the mixture around the outer boundary of the circle and on the heads of the assembled witches.

The nudity of the coven, the Great Rite ceremony, with the ceremonial binding and whipping of the initiate, truly reflect on an immoral group whose origins are definitely satanic. One worshiper said:

> *The Devil made them believe him to be the true God, and that the joy which the witches had at the Sabbath was the prelude of much greater glory.*

Witches attempted to imitate the church in many ways including an imitation of the Sabbath.

GROWTH OF SATANISM

**Satanism
Closely Aligned
With
Witchcraft**

It is estimated that in Great Britain at least **one in every 20 persons** has some relation with the occult world in one form or another. In the Ozark hill country of the United States, the ceremony of initiating a witch ends with the recitation of the Lord's Prayer backwards!

Closely aligned with witchcraft is **Satanism**. The root ideas of modern Satanism go far back beyond the 20th century to the Gnostic sects. The Greek word gnosis means **knows**. The

**Claiming
To Have
Secret
Knowledge**

Gnostic was <u>not</u> God–centered but, rather, <u>self</u>–centered. Gnostics were very prevalent in the second century. They claimed "to know" the great <u>secrets</u> of religion and life.

Satanists believe that God is evil and the enemy of Satan whose evil is "good." They believe that the Prince of Darkness is the true Lord of Light, Lucifer, "light bearer." As this age draws to a close, Satan will once again become very active, with himself and his demons entering human bodies and controlling personalities.

Satan is not dead. **He still has great powers!** Christians who fail to abide in Christ on a moment by moment basis may find their effectiveness as a Christian destroyed, should they yield to the Satanic temptations of this age.

No, witches do not ride on brooms. They are subtle, friendly; some are even beautiful and enticing! You may find them at your place of employment, in your neighborhood, and perhaps even teaching Sunday School [1 Peter 5:8].

Be on guard! For Satan is a master deceiver!

9

THE MYSTICAL ROSICRUCIANS

A FALSE CLAIM AND NO RESURRECTION

**Fraternity
Of The
Rosy Cross**

The Rosicrucians are one of many occult groups which claim to be guardians of "hidden knowledge." With their mysticism they fulfill the aims of the New Age Movement in denying the true God and seeking a One World government.

The Rosicrucians built their humanistic cult on the legend of <u>Christian Rosenkreuz</u>, founder of the <u>Fraternity of the Rosy Cross</u>.

The Rosicrucians [rose cross] cult was begun by Christian Rosenkreuz who was born in 1378 in Germany. He was the son of noble but poor parents. At the age of five he was placed in a monastery where he learned Greek and Latin.

As a youth he journeyed to the Middle East and remained for a while at Damascus. At 16 he learned of some "Wise Men" at Damacar in Arabia. It is claimed that these "wise men" warmly welcomed him as a long lost brother. Rosenkreuz learned Arabic and was able to translate a secret book, the <u>Liber M</u>, into Latin. He spent three years there.

From Damacar, Rosenkreuz went to Egypt and two years later left for Spain. Disappointed that he was not enthusiastically welcomed in Spain, he returned to Germany where he began to enlarge his philosophies.

**Three Monks
And A
Secret
Society**

It was there that **three monks** from his old monastery joined him. They became his disciples. They pledged to keep secret all that they learned from him. However, so that their successors could carry on the Fraternity of the Rosy Cross, they recorded everything in a manuscript book. The monks are listed simply by initials: G.V., I.A., and I.O.

And so this Fraternity of the Rosy Cross began . . . with four members. Eventually others joined: R.C. [his nephew], G.G., P.D. and finally I.A. and Brother B. All eight members were unmarried and pledged to chastity. They turned out an entire library of books. With their task completed they decided to go their various ways. They set up a number of guidelines:

1. None of the members were to exercise any profession except that of <u>medicine</u>. They were not to accept payment.

2. No distinctive dress was to be worn.

3. They would meet annually.

4. Each member was to look out for a person worthy to succeed him.

5. The initials R.C. were to be their seal and their password.

6. The identity of the fraternity was to remain a closely–guarded secret for 100 years.

THE SECRET BURIAL
[AND THE 7–SIDED VAULT]

**"In 120 Years
I Shall
Come Forth"**

When the first member died [R.C. Rosenkreuz's nephew], it was decided the burial places of the members should be secret. Soon afterward Rosenkreuz called the remaining six together and supposedly prepared his own symbolic tomb.

Apparently no one knew where or when Christian Rosenkreuz died . . . although he was supposed to have lived until the age of 106. His body was accidentally discovered 120 years after his death when one of the Brothers in the occult order decided to make some architectural alterations in their Temple.

While making his alterations, the Brother discovered a memorial tablet. On the tablet were the names of the earlier members of the Order. He attempted to remove the memorial tablet and in so doing some stones and plaster were broken disclosing a door concealed in the masonry. Upon the door was mystical writing which these Brothers interpreted to read:

"In 120 years I shall come forth."

They entered the vault. It had <u>seven sides</u> and <u>seven corners</u>, each side five feet wide and eight feet high. The sun had never penetrated this tomb but they claimed it was brilliantly illuminated by a mysterious light in the ceiling. In the center was a circular altar. On the altar were brass plates engraved with strange characters.

In each of the seven sides was a small door which, upon being opened, revealed a number of boxes filled with books, secret instructions and a record of Rosenkreuz's life and travels.

Further investigating, they moved the circular altar and lifted the heavy bronze plate. Much to their surprise they found the body of Christian Rosenkreuz still in a perfect state of preservation. In his hand he held a manuscript copy of **Liber T**, written with letters of gold on parchment. This manuscript was considered by them their bible. They then replaced the bronze plate on the coffin, closed the door of the vault and sealed it.

This legend was printed in 1615 A.D. in *Fama Fraternitatis*. This book was soon followed by another book that invited the readers to join this brotherhood movement.

THE LETTER AND THE CROSS

The Fair And Glorious Lady Delivers A Letter

Several other books followed and the story was enlarged. It tells of Rosenkreuz who on the eve of Easter was meditating when a "fair and glorious lady" appeared and delivered a letter, sealed with a cross inviting him to a royal wedding. The next morning he put on white garments, put <u>four roses</u> in his hat and made his way to a castle, being tested along the way.

He witnessed the royal marriage, was invested with the **Order of the Golden Fleece,** and claimed to have discovered the King's secret books of

Illustration at left is the Caduceus. Caduceus is the Latin word for a herald's staff of office. It is associated with the Greek god Hermes, the messenger of the gods. It represents an emblem of power (the wand) combined with wisdom (the snakes).

Symbol at right is the Tau Cross. This cross was inscribed on the forehead of every person admitted into the mysteries of Mithras. This symbol is preserved in modern Masonry under the symbol of the T square.

Doubt has always existed as to whether the name *Rosicrucian* came from the symbol of the rose and cross. Some scholars believe this was merely a blind to deceive the uninformed. They state that Rosicrucian is not derived from the flower but from the word *Ros*, which means *dew*. *Ras* means *wisdom* while *Rus* is translated *concealment*.

Rosicrucians claim that those who join their fraternity will learn the undreamed—of—secrets and wonders concerning the hidden workings of Nature.

wisdom. The author of this fantasy was Johann Valentin Andreae. Gradually the enthusiasm that this new order had created began to fade.

THE GOLDEN DAWN

He Saw Himself As a New Messiah!

A by–product of this cult was The Golden Dawn, founded in 1887 by 3 members of the Rosicrucian Society in England. A clergyman bought some old manuscripts from a bookshop. With the manuscripts was an old letter which said that anyone wanting to decipher the text should communicate with S.D.A. [Sapiens Donabitur Astris] through a Fraulein Anna Sprengel. This they did and the Golden Dawn's rituals were written by W.B. Yeats and MacGregor Mathers.

Mathers became increasingly occupied with black magic and sent Aleister Crowley to take over the London lodge. Crowley was violently hostile to Christianity and saw himself as Messiah of a new religion. He eventually came to America.

ENTER THE MASONS

Frank C. Higgens, a modern Masonic symbolist, writes:

> Dr. Ashmole, a member of this fraternity [Rosicrucian], is revered by Masons as one of the founders of the first Grand Lodge in London.[2]

[2]*The Secret Teachings of All Ages*, Manly P. Hall, 1928, p. 139.

**Based On
Superstition**

The Rosicrucians were a secret society based on superstition and occult practices. Most Masons deny there is any link between their fraternity and that of the Rosicrucians. This now brings us to perhaps the most controversial of the current secret societies, the Masons.

10

FREEMASONRY . . . ITS SECRETS AND SYMBOLS

A CONFUSED THEOLOGY THAT PROMOTES HUMANISM

Embraces All Religions

Freemasonry [or Masonry] is the name of one of the largest and oldest fraternal organizations in the world. Its full name is <u>Ancient Free and Accepted Masons</u>.

Masons today say their aims include the promotion of brotherhood and morality among its members. Men of any religious persuasion may join the Masons. Roman Catholics seldom join because it is against church doctrine to do so. Only avowed atheists may not become Masons.

Freemasonry has been defined as " . . . a system of morality veiled in allegory and illustrated by symbols."

For some, Freemasonry is merely an exclusive club with some secret rituals and camaraderie over a meal. For others, however, Freemasonry's rituals and teachings have a deeper, more spiritual content. Yet Freemasonry is <u>neither</u> a religion nor can it be considered a substitute. Basically it embraces all forms of religion.

MASONIC EMBLEMS

32nd Degree Mason

Mystic Shrine

33rd Degree Mason

Master Mason

George Washington, wearing the regalia as a member of the Masons, laid the cornerstone of the United States Capitol in Washington, D.C. in 1793.

Signs And Passwords

Originally the Lodges came into being wherever masons assembled for large scale building works. For a mason to be employed as a professional he was required to know certain <u>signs</u> and <u>passwords</u> that would identify his professional status.

Later the Speculative Freemasons took over. Speculative Masons were those who were <u>not</u> masons by profession but simply a group of men interested in a secret society.

ENGLISH ORIGINS

Famous People Among Its Members

In 1717, four fraternal lodges united under the Grand Lodge of England. Masons today accept this move as the beginning of their society. The Order quickly spread. It included George Washington, Benjamin Franklin, Frederick the Great of Prussia,Wolfgang Mozart and Voltaire.

In 1721, representatives of sixteen Lodges commissioned Dr. James Anderson to prepare a booklet which became known as <u>Anderson's Constitutions</u>. Anderson was a minister of the Church of Scotland!

Freemasonry rapidly expanded in Europe. In France a number of the Masonic sects dabbled with magic and occultism. In Germany some were called Order of the Gold and Rosy Cross [Rosicrucians]. In England, during the 1880's, the famous magical society, the <u>Merimetic Order of the Golden Dawn</u> adopted most of the Masonic grades.

It is interesting to note that Benjamin Franklin was originally hostile to Freemasonry. However, he did become a Mason in 1731 and remained devoted to the cause until his death in 1790. George Washington was Master of his Lodge when he became the first President of the United States in 1789.

THE FIRST RITUALS

An Elaborate Hierarchy

There is no single Grand Master in the United States. Instead each State has a Grand Lodge.

Freemasons meet in an elaborately furnished Lodge room. When a man enters the Masons, he joins a **Blue Lodge**. Members of the Blue Lodge may hold three degrees:

1. Entered Apprentice is the first degree.
2. Fellowcraft is the degree that follows.
3. Master Mason is the third degree.

Each degree in Masonry is supposed to teach a moral lesson. To earn a degree, a Mason must learn the lessons and participate in a ceremony that illustrates them. The Mason can then, after achieving the first three degrees, move on to receive further degrees in either or both of the two branches of advanced Masonry: the Scottish Rite and the York Rite.

THE SCOTTISH RITE

In the Scottish Rite, a Mason may advance through 29 more degrees. Thus the first degree of the Scottish Rite is actually the <u>fourth degree</u> in Masonry. The highest is the 33rd degree, which is an honorary degree. A 33rd degree Mason is sometimes called <u>Sovereign Grand Inspector General</u>.

THE YORK RITE

If a Mason selects to advance in the York Rite, degrees include among others: Mark Master, Royal Master and Super–Excellent Master. The 3 highest degrees are called: Knight of the Red Cross, Knight of Malta and <u>Knight Templar</u> [which is the highest].

INCOMPATIBLE WITH CHRISTIANITY

You Cannot Serve Two Masters!

On the surface, membership in the Masons would seem like a worthy contribution of time. Much of its work is in the social and constructive realm. Many Masons are members of Bible-believing Churches. They, unfortunately, are unaware of the basic ideologies of Masonry that make it incompatible with Christianity. One cannot serve two masters!

THE SECRET CEREMONY

In an initiation ceremony, the one to be initiated removes his tie and jacket and lays aside his money. The symbolism here is that Masons accept one regardless of wealth or lack of it.

Interconnected Organizations
AFFILIATED WITH THE MASONS . . .

Presently the number of Masons in the United States is twice that of the rest of the world. About 1 out of every 12 American males is a Mason, according to World Book Encyclopedia, 1969 edition. volume 13, p. 210. World membership is in the millions.

Interconnected organizations include:

1. **Order of De Molay**
   An organization of young men between the ages of 14 and 21. Since its founding in 1919, De Molay has initiated more than 2 1/2 million members. Members must be recommended by two chapter members or a senior De Molay or a Master Mason, The De Molay Order was founded in Kansas City in 1919. Its name was taken from Jacques De Molay who was the last Grand Master of the Knights Templars a famous group of French crusaders. The ritual for the De Molay Order includes secret ceremonies. International headquarters are in Kansas City, Missouri.

2. **International Order of the Rainbow for Girls**
   Another character building organization for girls 12 to 20. Members need not be related to a Mason, but must be recommended by a member of the Masonic Order or of the Eastern Star The Order has some 275,000 active members.

3. **International Order of Job's Daughters**
   This is for girls 12 to 20 who are relatives of Masons or of persons affiliated with a Masonic organization (called bethels) and an active membership of over 115,000.

4. **Order of the Eastern Star**
   This is a fraternal organization of Master Masons and their wives, widows, mothers, daughters and sisters. It supports charitable projects. It was founded in 1876. The Eastern Star has about 3 million members in 14 countries Its headquarters are in Washington, D.C.

5. **Ancient, Arabic Order of Nobles of the Mystic Shrine**
   This Masonlc order admits members who are at least 32nd–degree Masons in the Scottish Rite or Knights Templar in the York Rite.

6. **Daughters of the Nile**
   Wives of the Mystic Shrine members are members of this exclusive woman's group.

**A Secret
Ceremony**

He is then led into a room blindfolded. During the course of the ceremony the candidate swears a solemn oath not to reveal Freemasonry's secrets. The blindfold is removed. The candidate is then shown certain handgrips and signs and told certain secret words which are supposed to refer to the symbolical building of King Solomon's temple. He is then presented with a 24–inch gauge and a gavel. The 24–inch gauge represents the 24 hours of the day which are supposed to be divided into prayer, work, refreshment and helping a friend.

Much of Masonry centers around Solomon as the Master Builder. The Masonic legend of the building of Solomon's Temple does **not** in every particular parallel the Bible version.

Masonry through its origins and secret rituals seeks to become a religion in the university of life. A man goes through preliminary tests of initiations. We will see that Masonry attempts to have a form of godliness.

PSEUDO–BIBLE THEOLOGY

**Abounds
In
Symbolism**

The one being initiated into Freemasonry is instructed in the most "sacred," the most secret and supposedly the most enduring of all Mysteries . . . the mystery of **symbolism**. Solomon's Temple is intertwined in the myth to give it a quasi–Bible background.

Tarot cards are a set of playing cards bearing pictures of certain traditional allegorical figures and are used in fortune telling. They were used by ancient Egyptians and by Knights Templars from the Saracens [Moslems during the age of the Crusades about the 12th century]. They became a vital element in the Rosicrucian symbolism and had definite Masonic interest also.

Venturing Into Ritual Magic

A.E. White, born in 1857 in Brooklyn, made two ventures into ritual magic. He passed through the grades of the First Order of the Golden Dawn occult society. From the wealth of information he picked up he wrote that there are certain indications which point to a possible connection between Masonry and Rosicrucianism. Elias Ashmole [a Rosicrucian] was one of the founders of the first Grand Lodge in London. He was initiated into Freemasonry in 1646.

Dr. Gerard Encausse [better known as "Papus,"] studied both magic and occultism. In his book Tarot of the Bohemians, he wrote:

> We must not forget that the Rosicrucians were the Initiators of Leibnitz and founders of actual Freemasonry through Ashmole.

And so another link was forged!

ANCIENT ORIGINS CLAIMED

In several early Masonic manuscripts [Harleian, Sloane, Lansdowne] . . . it is claimed that the craft of initiated builders [Masons] existed <u>before</u> the Flood of Noah's day, and that its members were employed in the building of the <u>Tower of Babel</u>!

A Masonic Constitution dated 1701 refers to Genesis 4:16–24. From the line of Cain (through Methushael) was born Lamech [Genesis 4:18]. From Lamech's marriage to two wives [Adah and Zillah] came 4 children:

To Adah was born Jabal and Jubal . . .

And to Zillah was born Tubalcain and a daughter, Naamah

[Genesis 4:20–22]

TWO PILLARS OF STONE

The "Mysteries" And The Two Pillars Of Stone

The Masonic Constitution relates that these four discovered the major crafts of the world [Weaving, Mathematics, Stonemasonry and Iron Work] from Two Pillars of stone. The one stone was called Laturus and the other Marbell.

According to Freemason symbolism, Enoch [the son of Cain], erected the two pillars of stone, bearing all the knowledge of the "Mysteries" that would be lost at the time of the Great Flood. In addition to these two pillars upon which Enoch supposedly engraved the secret teachings was a marble column on which he is said to have placed an inscription stating that a short distance away a priceless treasure would be discovered in an underground vault.

Freemasonry theology goes on to say that Enoch was translated from atop Mount Moriah. Such was the pledge to secrecy among ancient freemasonry that Pliny, a Roman writer in the 1st century A.D., reveals how one man bit out his own tongue rather than reveal the secrets while in prison.

THREE TEMPLES

**The Supposed
Three Temples
Of Solomon**

According to early Masonic teaching there are three Temples of Solomon:

1. The Grand House of the Universe in the midst of which sits the sun upon his golden throne.

2. The human body which is the Little House made in the image of the Great Universal House.

3. Soular House, an invisible structure.

Albert Pike, who studied the mystics, wrote:

> *Freemasonry is more ancient than any of the world's living religions . . .*
>
> *I came at last to see that the true greatness and majesty of Freemasonry consists in its symbols; and its symbolism is its soul.*

But Freemasonry goes far beyond just symbolism and is a part of a powerful world order.

Nesta Webster, in her book, *World Revolution, The Plot Against Civilization,* page 157, describes alliances between Illuminism [the Illuminati] and Freemasonry. She states that the 1848 French Revolution

> *. . . was the second great attempt of illuminzed Freemasonry to bring about a world conflagration.*

The origins of freemasonry go back many hundreds of years. In a sense, their theology is one of agnosticism. [An <u>agnostic</u> is a person who believes that the human mind <u>cannot know</u> whether there is a God]

Based On Humanism And Paganism

There is no doubt that Masonic organizations are secret organizations. Their secrecy extends from their special handshake to the many secret code words and symbolism.

As with most secret societies, their origins include lifting of rituals from other secret societies that flourished when Freemasonry began. These origins were certainly not Christian but were based more on <u>humanism</u> and <u>paganism</u>. There is no doubt that the Masonic Orders endeavor to do good works. Indeed this is part of their program.

CAN CONTROL GOVERNMENTS

A Conspiracy Of Control

In 1981, in Italy, the four–party coalition government of Prime Minister Arnaldo Forlani toppled. Forlani, a Mason, released a card file listing names of 963 members in the secret Masonic lodge designated "P2" [the P standing for the word "Propaganda"]. The list of alleged P2 members read like an honor roll of Italy. They were accused of attempting to form "a state within a state."

A COMPROMISING POSITION

A believer in Christ should not join <u>any</u> secret society! This includes Masonic orders! There are many opportunities for a Christian to do good works within the dedicated framework of Christian ministries. To be part of any secret order is compromising your position and greatly lessening your effectiveness in the outreach of the Gospel.

Not only that, it is sin!

Christ's Command!

Christ said in Matthew 5:34,37:

> *But I say unto you, Swear not at all . . .*
>
> *But let your communications be Yea, Yea: Nay, Nay:*
>
> *For whatsoever is more than these cometh of evil.*

Thus Christians ought not to swear at all, let alone needlessly to fraternal oaths and loyalties, but reserve such loyalty <u>only</u> for Christ.

Christ said to give to Caesar what was Caesar's, and to God what was God's [Matthew 22:21]. Thus before <u>Caesar</u> [government], we may swear on the Bible in a Court of Law or upon induction into military service. Other loyalties, however, belong to <u>God</u>. He then will at the judgment give forth the true "secrets" [Revelation 2:17].

Secret societies are just another link into the overall New Age Plan to water down Christianity as they strive for their final goal of a humanistic One World society.

11

THE ILLUMINATI ... REAL OR IMAGINED?

THE WEB OF SECRECY EXPANDS

The Master Deception

In recent years in Christian circles there have been hushed whispers about the **Illuminati** and their conspiracy to control the world.

Illuminati comes from the root word, <u>illuminate</u>. The basic meaning of "illuminate" is "to give light" <u>or</u> "one who is enlightened in mind and spirit."

The Illuminati are defined as "a people who have or profess to have special intellectual or spiritual enlightenment."

Satan is a master deceiver. He began as Lucifer, "Bearer of Light."

The name Illuminati or "enlightened one" is derived from this.

FOUNDING OF THE ILLUMINATI

The Order of the Illuminati was founded on May 1, 1776 by Dr. Adam Weishaupt.

Weishaupt was Professor of Canon Law at the University of Ingolstadt in Bavaria. Weishaupt, although born a Jew, was a convert to Roman

Adam Weishaupt (left) found the Order of Illuminati in 1776 as a secret organization. Baron Adolph Knigge (right) reorganized the Order along Masonic lines. Eventually he left the Order. Many see Trilateralists as following similar aims.

♦ Thursday, June 22, 1978   Philadelphia Inquirer   9-A

Trilateralists run world —world won't cooperate

By William Greider
Washington Post Service

WASHINGTON — W h e n David Rockefeller's Trilateral Commission came to Washington last week and called upon the Carter Administration, it was like the nest returning to the sparrows.

President Carter, an ex-trilateralist himself, greeted his former brethren in the East Room with praise so generous that it was mildly embarrassing to some.

"I was dumbfounded by some of the things he said," a Trilateral executive said. "I would love to get permission to quote him in our fundraising."

This is terribly off-the-record, like all Trilateral discussions, but Carter told the 200 movers and shakers from America, Western Europe and Japan that if the Trilateral Commission had been in business after World War I, the world might have canceled World War II.

Thus encouraged, the trilateralists heard from three other alumni,

those filling U. S. cabinet posts who count most in global matters—State, Defense and Treasury. A fourth star, National Security Adviser Zbigniew Brzezinski, the intellectual father of the Trilateral idea, canceled his briefing because of illness.

At least 18 top-level executives of the Carter Administration were drawn from the Trilateral membership. So was the foreign minister of Japan. So were the prime minister of France and the labor minister of West Germany. The present membership includes 12 former cabinet officers and top advisers of past U. S. administrations, from Kennedy's to Ford's.

The Trilateral Commission is a very heavy group consisting of bankers and corporate barons, fellow-traveling technocrats, promising politicians and a light sprinkling of trade unionists drawn from three continents.

This has stimulated much spooky theorizing about a Rockefeller shadow on world government, a floating

establishment conspiracy to run everything. In some circles of fervid political imagination, the "Trilateral connection" is shorthand for puppets on a string, responding to a secret agenda.

The reality, alas, is less dramatic. On paper, they run the world. But, in the flesh, the trilateralists get together and mostly talk about how the world ought to be run, if only the world would cooperate.

This humble little secret slipped out from under the mirror-paneled doors at L'Enfant Plaza Hotel here, where the trilateralists met for three days last week: The heavyweight members, despite their awesome economic clout, feel defensive, uneasy, unloved.

'A rich man's club'

"It's surprising," said one participant, "that these big, powerful, hefty tycoons would be so defensive. They are not terribly confident."

Catholicism. He became a Jesuit priest only to break with that order to form his own secret organization. One of the reasons for secrecy was to avoid attacks by the Bavarian Jesuits.

They Used
A
Secret Name

He began his secret order with five members. Each member of the order assumed a secret name. Weishaupt was called Spartacus [the leader of an insurrection of slaves in ancient Rome].

Weishaupt's chief assistant, Herr von Zwack, took on the name of Cato.

Weishaupt hoped to attract the German Freemasons but he was unsuccessful. Finally a few prominent citizens in Munich joined upon learning they would receive the mysterious title of "Areopagite."

THREE CLASSES OF SECRET SOCIETY

An Oath
Of
Obedience

In 1779 Weishaupt divided his secret organization into three classes:

> Novice
> Minerval
> Illuminated Minerval

Each candidate had to swear an oath to secrecy plus unconditional obedience to Weishaupt. One feature of their society was a most unusual system of <u>mutual espionage</u>. Every member spied on every other member.

Every month the Novice was required to deliver to Weishaupt a sealed letter which revealed every aspect of his relationship with his superior.

When the Novice was promoted to the Minerval grade a solemn initiation ceremony was performed. The Novice was taken at night to a dimly lit room. Here he learned certain secret signs and a password. He was allowed to know who else was in his Minerval grade but the identities of the Illuminated Minerval were not disclosed.

THE ULTIMATE AIMS

**These Goals
Are Now
Coming To Pass!**

By the time a member had reached the grade of Illuminated Minerval, he learned the ultimate aims of the Order:

1. Abolition of all ordered government
2. Abolition of private property
3. Abolition of inheritance
4. Abolition of patriotism
5. Abolition of all religion
6. Abolition of the family
   [via abolition of marriage]
7. Creation of a World Government

Weishaupt wrote to his chief assistant, Cato:

> *"The most admirable thing of it all is that the great Protestant and reformed theologians [Lutherans and Calvinists] who belong to our Order really believe they see in it the true and genuine mind of the Christian religion.*
>
> *Oh man, what can not you be brought to believe?"*

LURING THE UNSUSPECTING

**Building
An Army
Of
Followers**

Weishaupt knew how to lure unsuspecting people into his organization and once wrote:

> *These people swell our numbers and fill our
> treasury; get busy and make these people nib-
> ble at our bait . . . but do not tell them our se-
> crets.*
>
> *They must be made to believe that the low de-
> gree that they have reached is the highest.*

Thus it was that influential people of that day became Novices, but these never attained to the higher grades where the real aims of the Illuminati were known.

INFILTRATING FREEMASONRY

**A Planned
Alliance**

Weishaupt gradually infiltrated the Freemasons. On July 16, 1782 at the Congress of Wilhelmsbad, an alliance between Illuminism and Freemasonry was finally sealed. On that day the leading secret societies were infiltrated, and to some degree, united . . . more than 3 million members!

The most influential member of those who then became Masonic Illuminati was Baron Adolph Knigge [1725–96]. He assumed the pseudonym Philo. He was a first class organizer. Johann Goethe, the famous German poet and dramatist was among those that joined at that time. Knigge quarrelled with Weishaupt because of his anti-clerical stand and left the Order.

Eventually the Bavarian government banned

both the Illuminati and the Freemasons on March 2, 1785.

**Secret Plan
Uncovered**

Weishaupt was forced to leave the country. The Bavarian government heard four leading members of the Illuminati testify before a Court of Inquiry exposing the Satanic nature of its aims. A voluminous array of documents were found in Illuminati headquarters. The Bavarian government published them to warn all the other countries of Europe. The name of this document was: Original Writings of the Order and Sect of the Illuminati.

ILLUMINATI ARRIVES IN AMERICA

**Now Firmly
Established
In The
United States**

However, by this time 15 lodges of the Order of the Illuminati had been established in the 13 Colonies. This was before the Colonies were united and the Constitution adopted. In 1785, the Columbian Lodge of the Order of the Illuminati was established in New York City. Its members included Governor DeWitt Clinton, Clinton Roosevelt and Horace Greeley. A Lodge in Virginia was identified with Thomas Jefferson.

In 1797, Professor John Robison published <u>Proofs of a Conspiracy</u>. He warned the world of Illuminati infiltration into Masonic Lodges.

STRANGE BEDFELLOWS

An English woman, Frances "Fanny" Wright, came to New York in 1829 to give a series of lectures promoting the Women's Auxiliary of the Illuminati. She advocated the entire Illuminati program including Communism. She also spoke of equal opportunity and equal rights, atheism, free love and the emancipation of women. Clinton Roosevelt [an ancestor of Franklin D. Roosevelt], Charles Dana and Horace Greeley were appointed to raise funds for this new undertaking.

His Revealing Remarks About God!

Clinton Roosevelt wrote a book, *Science of Government*. In it he wrote:

> *. . . there is no God of justice to order things aright on earth;*
>
> *if there be a God, he is a malicious and revengeful being, who created us for misery.*

Adam Weishaupt died in 1830 at the age of 82. It is believed he rejoined the Catholic Church with a death–bed repentance.

The Order of the Illuminati was revived in Berlin in 1906 by Leopold Engel, at the request of Theodor Reuss. Reuss was engaged in several pseudo–Masonic activities.

Weishaupt was just another link in a continuous chain who sought to perpetuate secret societies for their own evil ends.

There are many conspiracies to undermine Christianity. To point to the Illuminati as the singular moving force would be to attach to it something that has no convincing foundation. Long before Adam Weishaupt was born, the symbol he incorporated [The All–Seeing Eye] had its origin in Babylon days.

Agents of Satan   There is a single force which seeks to destroy the world. The Order of the Illuminati is simply <u>one</u> of its servants. That force is Satan who was the Angel of Light, Lucifer.

12

THE ILLUMINATI AND THE ALL–SEEING EYE

Origins In Babylon!

Dr. Adam Weishaupt, founder of the Order of the Illuminati, adopted the All–Seeing Eye symbol at the time he founded his Order on **May 1, 1776.**

The symbol is a pyramid with its top triangular stone being an eye. This symbol is found on the back of a $1 United States bill. At the base of the pyramid is the date 1776. Many, in error, believe this refers to the date of the signing of the Declaration of Independence. This is not solely true. It refers also, according to many, to the date Weishaupt founded the Order of the Illuminati.

Although the pyramid on the American dollar with its 13 levels ties in with the 13 colonies, the original association was with ancient Egyptian and Babylonian mysticism. Thus, mystery surround the implications found in the Great Seal of the United States of America.

THE BIG BROTHER ALL–SEEING EYE

Note that the cornerstone is missing from the top of the pyramid. In its place, instead you will see the All–Seeing Eye.

The Big Brother Plan Of Control

Weishaupt's mutual spying system was an integral part of his program to keep his associates in line. The eye symbolized a Big Brother controlling his domain. Those who dismiss this idea say the eye in the Great Seal is the "all–seeing" eye of God. However, the words in Latin underneath the pyramid of the great Seal

Novus Ordo Seclorum

mean

New Secular Order

The words in Latin above the Great Seal

Annuit Coeptis

mean

Announcing the Birth

Put the two together and you get

Announcing the birth of a New Secular Order.

With the cornerstone supplanted by an all–seeing eye, any reference to Christ is absent.

In Ephesians 2:20 God's Word reveals:

Jesus Christ Himself . . . the chief cornerstone.

And in Mark 12:10 and Luke 20:17, Christ is described as:

The Stone which the builders rejected.

DESIGNS BEHIND THE GREAT SEAL

Born Out of Occult and Mysticism

Who was appointed to prepare The Great Seal of the United States of America?

On July 4, 1776 Thomas Jefferson and John Adams [both Masons] and Benjamin Franklin [Rosicrucian] were commissioned to design the seal. This occurred some 31 years before John Adams became aware of the Illuminati conspiracy.

At the time that the United States of America was founded, European mysticism was not dead. Careful analysis of the Great Seal discloses a mass of occult and Masonic symbols. One such symbol is the so–called American Eagle. In its initial Seal, the Eagle was actually the Phoenix bird, which resembles closely the Eagle.

The Egyptian Phoenix was represented as having the body of a man and the wings of a bird. The Phoenix was a symbol of regeneration. Its third eye had an occult function which was known by the ancient priesthood. The Phoenix, in mythology, was reborn out of its own dead self seven times seven. The Phoenix was a symbol also used by the Rosicrucians. In the Grand

**Strange
Origins**

Rosicrucian magic formula the pyramid is the center of its design and the phoenix also appears.

Napoleon and Caesar's zodiacal eagle of Scorpio are really Phoenixes. It is interesting to note that the All–Seeing Eye of the Illuminati is also seen in the meditation room of the United Nations in New York.

No one for certain can say that the Great Seal of the United States was created by those whose minds were evil. However, a great weight of evidence points to the fact that the Rosicrucians exerted tremendous influence in its creation. And the Seal does have occult significance!

The top illustration is the bird's head from the first Great Seal of the United States in 1782. The bottom illustration is the Great Seal of 1902. The bird in the first Seal bore little resemblance to that of the eagle. This first so-called eagle resembled the mythological phoenix of antiquity. The phoenix bird was the Egyptian symbol of regeneration. Thus, the new country (United States) rising out of the old (Great Britain).

13

ILLUMINATI INFLUENCE IN COMMUNISM

THE STRANGE THEOLOGY OF KARL MARX

The League Of the Just

After Adam Weishaupt died, Giuseppe Mazzini [an Italian revolutionary leader] was appointed as Director of the Illuminati. He held this position from 1834 to 1872. Shortly after Mazzini took control of the Illuminati an obscure intellectual joined one of the branch organizations of the Illuminati called the <u>League of the Just</u>. His name was <u>Karl Heinrich Marx</u>.

Karl Marx denounced his Jewish birth and the Christianity of his parents, who were converts. He thus embraced Atheism, and studied at the universities of Bonn and Berlin and planned to be a professor of history and philosophy. He wrote the book *Das Kapital* which became the bible of the Communist movement. He wrote it with the help of Friedrich Engels.

Marx had a sad personal life . . . much of it due to his own failures. His marriage resulted in six children. Three of his children died of starvation while infants. Two of his children committed suicide!

**Marx
Outlined
His Plan!**

It was in 1847 that Marx wrote what later became known as the *Communist Manifesto*.

A manifesto is a public declaration of motives and intentions. This book outlined the overall plans for the future which urged laborers to revolt and for the government to own all property. Marx was such an unknown at that time that his name did not even appear on this document until 20 years after it was first published.

THE *COMMUNIST MANIFESTO*

**Enter
Albert Pike**

The *Communist Manifesto*, which struck out at capitalism, was basically simply a rehash of the writings of Adam Weishaupt and his disciple, Clinton Roosevelt.

In this same period, Giuseppe Mazzini selected Albert Pike to head the Illuminati activities

Symbol at left is the Crux Ansata sometimes called the Onk. It combines the masculine Tau Cross with the feminine oval to symbolize the principles of generation. Illustration at right is Egyptian conception of creation. Much of this symbolism has continued through Freemasonry and other secret organizations.

in the United States. Albert Pike was born in Boston in 1809. He went to Harvard and later served as Brigadier–General in the Confederate Army.

Albert Pike was a genius who used his intelligence with evil intent. He could read and write in 16 ancient languages.

ADMIRER OF CABALA

**Plans
For
World Control**

Pike was an admirer of the secret Hebrew cult of Cabala [Qabbalism]. Pike at that time was head of the Ancient and Accepted Scottish Rite of Freemasonry. Mazzini, in a letter dated January 22, 1870, wrote to Pike:

> *We must create a super rite, which will remain unknown, to which we will call those Masons of high degree whom we shall select.*
>
> *With regards to our brothers in Masonry, these men must be pledged to the strictest secrecy.*
>
> *Through this supreme rite, we will govern all Freemasonry which will become the one international center, the more powerful because its direction will be unknown.*

This letter was published in the book *Occult Theocrasy* by Lady Queenborough, pages 208–209.

PIKE AND HIS COUNCILS

This secret organization was founded by Pike under the name of The New and Reformed Palladian Rite. Supreme councils were established in Charleston, South Carolina, in Rome and in Berlin.

**The Height Of
Secret Ritual**

<u>Palladism</u> is the cult of Satan in the inner shrines of a secret ritual to surpass all other secret rituals.

Albert Pike's most famous book is the 861 page *Morals and Dogma of the Ancient and Accepted Scottish Rite of Freemasonry*. It was published in 1871. In it, he writes:

> *The blind Force of the people is a force that must be economized, and also managed . . . it must be regulated by intellect.*

> *When all Forces are combined, and guided by the Intellect [the Illuminati], and regulated by the Rule of Right and Justice . . . the great revolution prepared for by the ages will begin to march.*

> *It is because Force is ill regulated, that revolutions prove failures.*

> [*Morals and Dogma*, pp. 1,2]

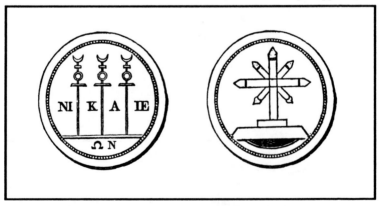

Symbolic cross emblems above were Standards of the pagan nations of the East.

On July 14, 1889 Pike issued this statement to the 23 Supreme Councils of the world.

**Revealing
Satan
As Their God!**

> *That which we must say to the crowd is: We worship a God, but it is the God one adores without superstition.*
>
> *To you, Sovereign Grand Instructors General, we say this, that you may repeat it to the Brethren of the 32nd, 31st and 30th degrees:*
>
> *The Masonic religion should be, by all of us initiates of the high degrees, maintained in the purity of the Luciferian doctrine.*

In 1871 Giuseppe Mazzini issued a remarkable letter in which he graphically outlined plans for **three** world wars. Until recently this letter was on display in the British Museum Library in London.

Albert Pike aided in making this plan known in the United States.

It was a blueprint for three world wars!

U S A. Copyright 1981 by Salem Kirban

ABIDING LOVE/ Goodbye My Sweetheart for just tonight, May God watch o'er you till morning light. From Heaven above, you'll find me waiting. With joy I'll sing my song of love. (This song Bill Sanders sings to his wife, Faye, in the book *666,** when he is led into the guillotine.)

And I saw the souls of those who had been beheaded because of the testimony of Jesus and because of the Word of God. and those who had not worshiped the beast or his image. and had not received the mark upon their forehead and upon their hand; and they came to life and reigned with Christ for a thousand years (Revelation 20:4).

---

*If you wish to order *666/1000* by Salem Kirban . . . see Order Form at back of this book.

14

THE THREE WORLD WARS

PLANNED OR COINCIDENCE?

**The Planning
Of Three
Global Wars!**

In the previous chapter we showed how Albert Pike's interlocking subordinate groups created a planned conspiracy.

The Mazzini–Pike plan was to control the world. How would this be accomplished?

This New Age plan was relatively simple. It called for, according to the writings of some, for the forces of Communism, Fascism, and the struggle for the Mid–East to foment <u>three</u> global wars and at least <u>two major revolutions</u>.

WORLD WAR 1

The **First World War** was to enable Communism to destroy the Czarist government of Russia and replace it with militant atheism. This came to pass and we now see the results of the overthrow.

WORLD WAR 2

The **Second World War** would be started by a

manipulation of the governments of Great Britain and Germany to start a world war.

**Communism's
Growth**

Hitler, however, accomplished this almost single handed, bringing on **World War 2**. After this war, Communism would then be in a position to destroy other governments and weaken religions. This also came to pass.

Russia controls most of Europe and the Gospel has been effectively suppressed in many nations. This atheistic movement has also successfully spread to China when China became closed to Christianity after World War 2.

WORLD WAR 3

**The Next War
Between
Islam and
Israel!**

The Mazzini–Pike blueprint also included a plan for a **World War 3**. This would begin by firing up the controversy between Judaism and the Moslem world. They hoped that the Zionists and Moslems would destroy each other and bring the rest of the world into a final conflict. This Armageddon would bring complete social, political and economic chaos.

To fill the void created by Armageddon would come World Government, headed by the Illuminati. The Illuminati are against both Christianity and atheism. They seek to destroy both and supplant it with Satan as their god, but by the name of Lucifer. In fact they do not accept the doctrine of Satanism. In the Illuminati doctrine, Lucifer is God and the doctrine of Satanism is a heresy. Lucifer is their God of Light. The

Christian God [Adonay] they state is the God of evil.

We Are Headed In That Direction!

In a letter now catalogued in the British Museum in London, Pike wrote to Mazzini regarding the final war [World War 3]:

> *Then everywhere, the people, disillusioned with Christianity, will receive the true light, that will follow the destruction of Christianity and atheism both conquered and exterminated at the same time.*

What about **World War 3**? If you carefully read current news events and see the alignment of nations it is not hard to understand that the third World War could be between forces united with Israel **against** the forces united with Communism and Islam.

Time Will Tell!

Is it possible that these secret groups, being in league with Satan as they are, actually [even without realizing it] have had revealed to them Satan's program in advance? If so, they have truly been Satan's prophets of coming doom! But there is even more to this tangled web of intrigue. For Satan's army is vast and he employs many puppets in an attempt to achieve his evil desires. Some of these little known emissaries include:

The GROUP / Secret financiers from England

The ORDER / World power builders from the U.S.

The NEW AGERS / Pawns in a One World Movement manipulated by both The Group and The Order.

More To Come   You will find more revealing information on these subtle conspirators in the next section of this book.

The
NEW AGE PLAN
of
WORLD CONQUEST!

The "Plan" began in 1975! It combines the forces of an international network of organizations and big business *plus* the television and print media. Its aim: To wipe out Christianity and establish a One World Religion headed by a False Christ. It seeks to achieve this goal by the year 2000!

PART THREE

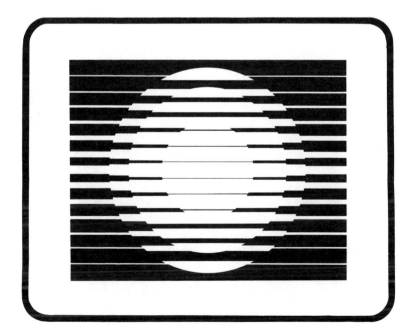

15

The Gathering Storm

SATAN'S FINAL FLING FOR FAME

**We Are Already
Seeing Signs!**

We are living in the Last Days just prior to the Rapture! There are many signs that indicate this!

We all can point to obvious signs such as the final alignment of nations, the breakdown of the family unit, the spreading scourge of AIDS, the stockpiling of nuclear weapons, the pollution of our atmosphere and the depletion of our resources.

An even surer sign is the rapid deterioration of the Church, particularly in the United States. We have become more concerned about building our own little religious empires, halls of granite that will attest to our abilities to raise millions of dollars, than the cause of Christ.

National TV ministries have spoon fed Christians on the milk of the Word. And as a result the majority of Christians are more concerned about their financial security and success than they are about the things of God.

WHAT'S IN IT FOR ME, LORD?

One Sunday the late Dr. Peter Marshall chose

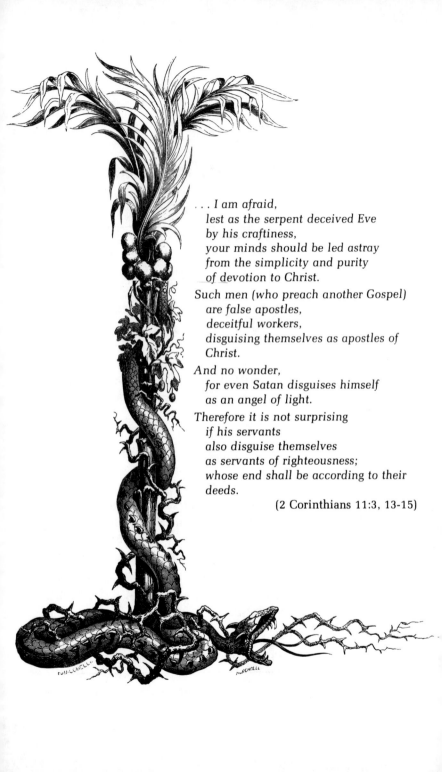

... I am afraid,
 lest as the serpent deceived Eve
 by his craftiness,
 your minds should be led astray
 from the simplicity and purity
 of devotion to Christ.

Such men (who preach another Gospel)
 are false apostles,
 deceitful workers,
 disguising themselves as apostles of
 Christ.

And no wonder,
 for even Satan disguises himself
 as an angel of light.

Therefore it is not surprising
 if his servants
 also disguise themselves
 as servants of righteousness;
 whose end shall be according to their
 deeds.

(2 Corinthians 11:3, 13-15)

for use in a church service the familiar hymn of consecration, "Take My Life and Let It Be."

He requested the congregation to give particular thought to the words:

> *Take my Silver and my Gold*
> *Not a mite would I withhold!*

Are We Really Dedicated Christians?

Explaining the practical sense of the words: "Not a mite would I withhold," he asked that all who could not sing this line with literal sincerity, refrain from singing it at all.

The effect was a dramatic commentary on the glib, thoughtless manner in which, all too often, we sing our hymns.

Hundreds of voices with organ accompaniment, sang vigorously up to the designated point. Then suddenly, there was only the sound of organ music.

Not a single voice ventured to so challenging a height!

Would you be able to sing?

How much more of an outflow of cash . . . even thousands of dollars perhaps . . . would there be if you were promised in return a time–share apartment, an investment that would bring you security at age 60, a healing miracle, or prosperity?

Most Christians in America are wrapped up in themselves. We pay out homage to the Gospel of self–esteem. And Satan laughs up his sleeve as he realizes his time has finally come!

**A
Dangerous
Detour!**

IT'S TIME
TO RESTORE SANITY IN THE CHURCH!

We as believers are facing a subtle danger. Some Christian leaders [knowingly or unknowingly] are carried away with the cheers of supporters to feel that they <u>personally</u> can resolve the world's problems. And with this attitude in mind they have become bogged down in the <u>quagmire of detour</u> in promoting **CAUSES** instead of **CHRIST**!

In 2 Chronicles 20:15, the Lord spoke through His servant, Jehosphaphat saying:

> *Be not afraid nor dismayed by reason of this great multitude; for the battle is not yours, but God's.*

Satan is no fool! Of all the fallen angels, Satan is the most clever. In fact, during the 1000 year Millennium . . . where people live 1000 years in comparative peace and safety [the ultimate in social security] Satan will still be able to deceive millions to follow him. You will want to read Revelation 20:7–10.

Satan realizes that when a person accepts Jesus Christ as his personal Saviour and Lord . . . that he, Satan, has lost that <u>war</u>! But Satan is determined he will not lose the intervening <u>battles</u>! If I could read Satan's mind, I would imagine him saying to himself:

> *So John Jones has accepted Christ . . . But I am going to defuse his zeal . . . I will detour his energies into non–productive or less productive channels and defuse his soul–winning passion.*

And that's what Satan is successful in doing!

A Tragic Transition

Are we devoting too much time and money to <u>causes</u> instead of <u>Christ</u>? Isn't it amazing how we can whip up millions of dollars and thousands of Christians to fight a cause or elect a political leader while the testimony of Christ is lost in the shadows of a faithful few who give what little they have to keep missionaries on the field! What has happened to the Church in the last 25 years?

<u>The Southern Baptists</u>
are fighting each other to determine whether or not the Bible is really the inspired Word of God . . . while many of their colleges are awash in liquor . . . and their church steps lost in a fog of cigarette puffing elders.

<u>The "Other Baptists"</u>
are determined to build the biggest churches, the biggest schools and get stuck on the theology of "get them saved and baptized into a Baptist church!"

<u>The Charismatics</u>
want to get everybody speaking in tongues, healed and prosperous while looking for new miracles, dreams and signs!

<u>The Bible Institutes</u>
want to de–emphasize the Bible and train students in computer technology and business administration

<u>The Bible Conferences</u>
want to become winter sport and summer

pleasure resorts teaching basketball, baseball and golf!

Is it any wonder Satan is jumping for joy!

Now that you may be good and mad at me . . . I trust I have gained your attention!

**Time
To Get Back
To Basics**

The comments on the previous page were not meant to include all churches, Bible schools or Bible conferences. There are many that are humble, dedicated and true to the Word of God. These comments were made simply to show you the very dangerous trend that is developing.

To me . . . this trend is the surest sign that we are living in the Last Days.

It is a sign of the gathering storm that suddenly, one day soon, will engulf us!

While there is still time . . . let us realign our priorities!

Forget about . . .

Building a bigger church
Striving for the biggest college
Teaching computer technology
Having camps for winter and summer sports

and let's get back to the basic essentials of the Word of God!

Christians today are basically feasting on a sawdust diet. As a result, we are more interested in psychology and prosperity, castles and causes, experiences and the economy.

Satan is extremely successful in defusing our zeal for Christ and detouring our efforts toward

nonproductive areas. And many will fall vic-
tim to this gathering storm!

16

STEPS TO A ONE WORLD GOVERNMENT

**WHILE THE WORLD SLEEPS . . .
POWER SEEKERS SCHEME**

**CFR . . .
The Council
On
Foreign
Relations**

George Bush, when running for the Presidency in the New Hampshire primaries in February, 1988 . . . was asked about the Council on Foreign Relations, known as the **CFR**.

Laughingly he replied that he was glad someone asked him that question and said, in effect, that there are always people who think that the CFR is some kind of conspiracy. He said this was ridiculous . . . it was just a group of businessmen from various free world countries who are striving for a better world. He also stated he was no longer a member of the CFR.

The CFR is actually only a very small link in a much greater chain of conspiracy. Actually it is on the outer circle of the one world conspiracy plan. They have about 2500 members [The Trilateral Commission has only 200 members worldwide!]

The CFR and the Trilateral Commission membership is not secret. This in itself indicates that they are not the major conspirators for a One World Government. They are the sounding boards for which ideas of world domination are first expressed.

DESIGNS ON POWER

CFR Goals Already Accomplished!

The Council on Foreign Relations was formed in 1921 when it became evident that the United States was not going to join the League of Nations. Its founder was Colonel Edward House.

House was a British–educated son of a financier who had British financial interests in the United States. House became President Wilson's right-hand–man and emerged as virtually "President–in–Control." House had two pet projects he wanted to ram through:

1. A Central Banking System
2. Graduated Income Tax

He was successful in seeing that both were adopted into law. It was House who brought into being the Federal Reserve Act, which benefited international bankers. House was an admirer of <u>Karl Marx</u>!

While George Bush sought to convince inquiring reporters that the CFR was just some sort of business fraternity . . . let's look at the record.

In Study No. 7, published by the Council on Foreign Relations on November 25, 1959 and in further statements, the following was recommended:

Edward M. House (left) was President Wilson's closest friend and trusted advisor. House was a front for the "internationalists" who sought a central bank and income tax. His ultimate aim was socialism.

President Wilson sought to push through the League of Nations treaty. In effect, it would have surrendered national sovereignty. Today, once more, there is a combined effort among the money manipulators to achieve this same end. Could this be the End Time conspiracy that ushers in Antichrist?

Dangerous Aims

1. **General**

[a] Build a new international order . . . including states [nations] labeling themselves as "Socialist." [b] Our broader and ultimate objective . . . is a universal community of nations.

2. **United Nations**

Maintain and gradually increase the authority of the UN.

Much more is involved including a recommendation of secret negotiations with Russia on disarmament, increased foreign aid with no strings attached and recognition of Red China. All this has now come to pass!

THE INVISIBLE GOVERNMENT

The Growing Threat To Freedom!

The CFR has been called "the invisible government." It is interesting to note that members of the CFR have at one time or another staffed almost every key position of every administration since that of Franklin Delano Roosevelt! Yet most Americans are unaware that such an organization exists!

The CFR issues a quarterly magazine, *Foreign Affairs.* Let's look at one of the most important policy articles published in this magazine. A 14–page article appeared in the January 1973 issue of *Foreign Affairs,* pages 286–299. The article is titled, "The Changing Essence of Power."

The article is quoted in part. We are printing some of the direct quotes in boldface although

Trends
Toward
Complete
Control

boldface type does not appear in the original article.

> Today's political flux features on its diplomatic surface three interacting trends: a disintegration of cold–war coalitions, the rise of non–security issues to the top of diplomatic agendas, and a diversification of friendships and adversary relations.
>
> These surface movements are the expression of deeper currents, **which if appropriately exploited by providential statesmanship, could fundamentally alter the essence of world politics, changing the structures and ingredients of power itself . . . .**
>
> What, then, becomes to today's great powers, especially the two superpowers? How would they stand under new criteria of power? . . .
>
> The nine or more members of the European Economic Community [Common Market countries], when acting as a unit on particular international issues, could well emerge as **an equally powerful unit in world politics.**[3]

Here we paraphrase for brevity.

> 1. The United States and Russia must not utilize their military superiority as a bargaining advantage.
>
> 2. The wealthiest countries [U.S., etc.] must stop attempting to maintain "spheres of dominance, or even to maintain permanent extended alliance systems."
>
> 3. The United States and other leading nations should actively cooperate with countries in "rival ideological blocs."

---

[3]Now can you see how the United States of Europe will become supremely powerful with Antichrist as its head.

**Steps
Toward
Antichrist**

4. A world system should correct any imbalances through a world political economy.

5. New sets of representative institutions will need to be elaborated and empowered on regional and global bases to insure that all communities affected have a fair say over how these common goods [from the ocean, the atmosphere and outer space] are used. [Paraphrasing ends here]

The article continues:

> *There appears to be growing support for policies that would reduce the foreign commitments of the U.S., bring the American military personnel home, trim the defense budget and cut foreign military and economic assistance . . .*

Both the Council on Foreign Relations and The Trilateral Commission seek to reduce nationalism [old fashioned patriotism] and encourage in its place internationalism . . . a One World society.

The New Age plan of world conquest is already at work. While it began in the early 1920's with the emergence of the Council on Foreign Relations . . . it was further encouraged in 1973 by the creation of The Trilateral Commission by David Rockefeller. This was the groundwork.

Then, in 1975 the New Age Movement let out all the stops in the final stage of their Plan to wipe out Christianity and establish a One World Religion headed by a False Christ!

17

WORLD WAR 1 and WORLD WAR 2

WHAT THE HISTORY BOOKS DON'T TELL YOU

Enter The Rothschilds

In 1773 in a goldsmith shop in Frankfurt, Germany, Mayer Amschel Bauer [wealthy at age 30] invited twelve other wealthy and influential men to meet with him to develop a Plan of conquest.

He encouraged them to work together as one unit and pool their resources. Their aim: to control the natural resources and wealth of the world. By amassing their wealth they could use this as a leverage to create adverse economic conditions.

They adopted a plan which included:

1. *Use of any means to reach this goal was justified.*

2. *Our right lies in force!*

3. *The power of our resources must remain invisible.*

4. *Alcohol, drugs, moral corruption must be used to corrupt youth of all nations.*

But there was much more to this Plan!

5. *Wars should be directed so that the nations engaged on both sides would become further*

in debt . . . and obligated to the "Wealth Manipulators."

6. *Candidates to public office must follow our commands.*

7. *Our wealth will be directed to control the media to serve our propaganda purposes.*

8. *Part of our method of operation to achieve a One World government will be to trigger panics and financial depression.*

Making Millions By Bankrupting Nations

Mayer Amschel Bauer later changed his name to Mayer Amschel **Rothschild.** Frederick Morton, in his book, *The Rothschilds,* wrote:

> For the last 150 years the history of the House of Rothschild has been to an amazing extent the backstage history of Western Europe. Because of their success in making loans not to individuals, but to nations, they reaped huge profits . . . Someone once said that the wealth of Rothschild consists of the bankruptcy of nations.[4]

Mayer Amschel Rothschild's first financial success was in his manipulation of the London exchange during the Battle of Waterloo [June 18, 1815]. He withheld information on Napoleon's defeat and gained control of the Bank of England.

In the early 1900's, European countries had large standing armies. They had modern weapons and a universal military service. But their economy could not support the enormous expenditures to keep this going.

---

[4]Frederick Morton, *The Rothschilds,* (Fawcett Publishing Company), New York, 1961, p. 36.

One day in the Tribulation Period you will need proper identification to withdraw or deposit money in your bank. That identification will be an invisible mark either on the back of your right hand or on your forehead!

Each teller position will have a Laser Identification Beam that will be used to make your mark visible. You will need this even to cash your Social Security check!

Quite possibly, you may even have to supply your Worldwide Money Card. A tiny computer chip on your Money Card can contain over 10,000 transistors and store your complete life history and credit record! Can you imagine the power that international bankers and Antichrist will have over the individual with this data at their instant control!

Financing Both Sides!

The money manipulators, anxious to reap their huge profits, went to work pitting nation against nation. It was in this era that the Federal Reserve System came into operation [1914]. One of their first moves at that time was to lend European allies **$25 Billion!**

Meanwhile, agents of the Rothschilds conglomerate were financing the Kaiser while other of their representatives were aiding the Bolshevik Revolution in Russia . . . paving the way for the rise of communism [sowing the seeds for World War 3].

Thus the Plan was working—wars were being created so that forces on both sides would incur debt. The money manipulators would finance the debt to these nations, reaping huge profits!

THE MEETING

A Secret Plan

In July, 1927, directors of three great central banks met in Europe. They represented the Bank of England, the New York Federal Reserve Bank and the German Reichsbank. It became apparent afterwards that one of the goals was to get gold moved out of the United States. This movement of gold out of the United States helped trigger the depression of 1929–31.

By 1928, the League of Nations had been able to get the nations of Europe back on the gold standard. And the Federal Reserve [after secret meetings with the heads of foreign central banks] transferred **$500 Million** in gold to Europe!

You are looking at the Common Market Headquarters in Brussels, Belgium. Antichrist, quite possibly, could become the head of this union of 10 nations. Turn this page. You will note this building is shaped in the form of a stylized cross!

SOWING THE SEED FOR WORLD WAR 2

**The
Money
Manipulators'
Greed
For Power**

The United States and European Allies who had been manipulated into World War 1 were now loaded with a fantastic debt. This is exactly the position the international bankers wanted!

To reduce this debt they made demands on the German people for reparations [restoration of money] that were economically unreasonable!

The treaty was called <u>The Treaty of Versailles</u>. The Germans initially refused to sign this treaty but it was finally signed by two obscure Germans who were relatively unknown. The final amount of money demanded from Germany was 132 Billion Gold Marks. This sum, the equivalent of $35 Billion was soon pronounced by various Western economists to be more than Germany could possibly contrive to pay. It was this unreasonable demand that would prepare the stage for the seeds of revolt that would end in World War 2.

It is interesting to note that, in the 1920's, John D. Rockefeller, Jr. gave France $2.8 Million to restore the Versailles Palace where this treaty was signed. Versailles is a city in northern France.

The money manipulators had succeeded in creating World War 1, opening up Russia for the birth of communism,and preparing the stage for World War 2.

Germany, weakened by unusual financial demands, signed a treaty with Russia in 1922

Inflation Made A Hitler Possible!

What were the factors that made a Hitler possible?

1. The currency became worthless!
   · Inflation is making the U.S. dollar lose much of its purchasing power!

2. $6 Billion in foreign loans collapsed!
   · The United States gives some $10 Billion in foreign aid annually!

3. 6 Million Germans were unemployed!
   · Today the United States has over 7 Million unemployed!

4. Unfair taxes, power of the great trusts, big money monopolies and power of the banks all were targets of Hitler's speeches!
   · Today, the United States faces similar problems. AT&T earnings in 1980 hit an all time high ($6 Billion) while Exxon, the oil giant made 1980 profits of $5.66 Billion! These profits were earned while the average person struggled to pay soaring oil and gas bills and put food on their table!

[Treaty of Rapallo]. The German army dispatched officers and technicians to give instruction to the Red Army.

It is interesting to note that both Germany and Russia were in the League of Nations.

CREATING A COUNTERFEIT CHRIST

**Hitler
A Pawn
In The Hands
Of
Financiers**

During World War 2, CBS correspondent William Shirer wrote in his Berlin Diary:

> *I got my first glimpse of Hitler as he drove by the Würtemberger Hof to his own headquarters . . . I got caught in a mob of about 10,000 hysterics who jammed the moat in front of Hitler's hotel shouting,* **"We want the Führer!"**

> *I was literally shocked at the faces, especially those of the women.*

> *When Hitler finally appeared on the balcony for a moment . . . they looked at him as though he were the Messiah.*

How could Adolph Hitler, an obscure paperhanger from Austria, become so powerful a leader in Germany? In 1919, Adolph Hitler had joined the German Workers Party. It was supported by financiers who were members of The Thule Society. Inner core members of this Society were Satanists and practiced Black Magic.

In 1921, Hitler met with Admiral Schroder who was commander of the German Marine Corps. This led to a coalition of a circle of financier friends which included the following: Baron Kurt von Schroder, J.H. Stein who was Hitler's personal banker, and Hjalmar Schacht, Hitler's Finance Minister.

Interlocking Financial Interests!

These men had interlocking financial interests with London bankers and also with prominent Americans. On January 4, 1933 and June 11, 1934, Hitler and his aides met with very well known British and American leaders to arrange loans to finance his cause.

Once Hitler had served the purpose of the money manipulators . . . creating a world war and debt by opposing nations . . . these same bankers

A rare and revealing photograph shows Adolf Hitler accepting a bouquet of roses from a child. Hitler knew how to appeal to the German people! And Antichrist will use the same techniques!

sought to assassinate him. They were unsuccessful. The mastermind of this plot was Axel von dem Bussche. He was the grandson of a partner in the J.P. Morgan Company and linked to international financiers in both England and the United States.

Managed Conflicts

Several major Foundations in the United States have benefited by these "managed conflicts." Through the influence of the money manipulators, after World War 2, Germany was split into two nations. This was to prepare the seeds of conflict for World War 3 . . . pitting the Soviet Union against the European nations and eventually even the United States. This, the money barons hope, will bring about a One World Order!

How did Hitler ever manage to rise in power in Germany? Is the United States caught in a pattern that will eventually produce a counterfeit Christ?

Germany fell in 1918 and World War 1 ended. But in 20 years history would repeat itself. Only this time. the remedy would be far more costly.

The Allied victors made the mistake at the Versailles Peace Conference of demanding a tremendous price out of the Germans.

A man more subtle and more powerful than Hitler will arise!

18

A WORLD RELIGION FOR A NEW AGE

**THE 13–POINT
MASTER PLAN OF CONTROL**

**Seeking
A New Age
Messiah**

We hear a great deal about the New Age Movement. But few realize this is just an extension of what began in Babylon at the beginning of time.

Man wants to be his own god governed by his own rules and conquering the world as though it was a residence he created. And to head this system they want their own New Age Messiah!

One New Age writer wrote:

> *A World Religion for the New Age . . . is needed to meet the needs of thinking people . . . and to unify mankind.*

The New Age Movement has millions of followers throughout the world. They welcome into their fold most everyone . . . Buddhists, Secular Humanists, Satanists . . . in fact any religion. They do not welcome those who believe in Jesus Christ as their personal Saviour and Lord.

They state that Man does not need a Saviour, that man is evolving towards perfection.

THE PLAN FOR WORLD DOMINATION

**13–Point Plan
Of The
New Age
Movement**

In his book, *Dark Secrets of the New Age,* Texe Marrs outlined the 13–point Plan formulated by the New Agers.

1. A One World, New Age Religion and one world political and social order will be established.

2. The idolatrous religion of ancient Babylon in which mystery cults, sorcery, occultism and immorality flourished will be revived.

3. The Plan is to come to fullness when the New Age Messiah, the Antichrist, with the number 666 comes in the flesh to lead the unified New Age World Religion and oversee the new One World Order.

4. Spirit guides [demons] will help man inaugurate the New Age and will pave the way for the Antichrist.

5. "World Peace!", "Love!", and "Unity!" will be the rallying cries of the New Age Religion.

6. New Age teachings are to be taught in every sphere of society around the globe.

7. New Age leaders and their followers will spread the apostasy that Jesus in neither God nor the Christ.

8. All religions are to become an integral part of the New Age World Religion.

9. Christian principles must be discredited and abandoned.

**It's Time
For
Christians
To Wake Up!**

10. Children will be spiritually seduced and indoctrinated to promote New Age dogma.

11. Flattery will be employed to entice the world into believing man is divine god.

12. Science and the New Age World Religion will become one.

13. Christians who resist The Plan will be dealt with. If necessary, they will be exterminated and the world "purified."[5]

As you can see by this 13–point Plan . . . the New Age Movement is striving for:

1. A World Organization
2. A World Economy
3. A World Religion

The New Age Movement has tens of thousands of interlocking organizations propagating their humanistic theology.

Constance Cumbey, author of *The Hidden Dangers of the Rainbow* and *A Planned Deception*, should be given credit for her pioneering efforts to make Christians aware of the dangers of the New Age Movement. She stated that the New Age Plan includes a new world religion under Maitreya.

As early as 1931 New Age writers were writing that the world must go through a purification process that would brainwash Christians and eradicate those believers who refused this "education."

---

[5]Texe Marrs, Dark Secrets of the New Age (Crossway Books, 1987) P. 16, 17.

FIVE WAYS TO CONTROL YOUR LIFE!

Right now, the technology exists to:

1. Keep you from buying or selling. A laser marking system is already a fact!

2. Immediately determine your status. Within **5** seconds a computer can deliver a print-out revealing everything about you and your family, including whether you are a believer and (eventually) whether you contribute to right wing conservative groups and what church you attend!

3. Prevent your wife from conceiving. Contraceptive subdermal implants are *now* ready for the American market. These 6 implants would be placed under the skin of your wife's forearm in a fan-shaped pattern and would prevent her from conceiving for **six** years. The side effects will be nausea, headaches, irregular bleeding and blood tumors.[1]

4. Prevent you from withdrawing your own money from your bank or savings and loan. Computer technology makes it possible to single out believers and deny them the opportunity to withdraw funds . . . or limit them to a figure such as $25 per week!

5. Monitor your every activity and thought patterns! A computer chip (no larger than the size of your little fingernail) can be implanted under your skin. Such a device can transmit signals back to a Master computer terminal and chart your every activity. Sensing devices in the chip can record body changes that, when translated via computer techniques, can discern whether you have negative or positive thought patterns . . . and whether you have an aggressive or passive nature. And if your nature is aggressive and defiant . . . upon instruction, a Computer can trigger the *"spy implant"* to release a long-term tranquilizing drug that will make you subservient to the State!

While this technology, for the most part, is already here . . . it will not be implemented in full until the Tribulation Period. For the believer, that is one consolation as one can see, with this oppression, there will be no place to hide!

---

[1]*Medical World News*, February 16, 1981, p. 56.

1975 . . . YEAR OF BEGINNING

**Unveiling
"The Plan"**

Alice Bailey is the author of at least five books published by the Lucis Trust ["Lucis" is the Greek word for Lucifer].

Bailey revealed that her "hidden Masters" told her that beginning in 1975 the time would be ripe for open propagation of **The Plan**.

The Plan includes:

1. A universal credit card system

2. A universal tax

3. A universal draft

4. Outlawing of all present religious practices and symbols of orthodox Jews and Christians

One prominent New Age writer calls for the New Age to be ushered in by the year 2000.

New Agers believe that by merging all religions into one and establishing a One World government they will fulfill all man's dreams and climax his greatest hopes. Such fulfillment, they believe, will complete the "evolutionary plan" that lifts man to a divine status.

DRUGS • A.I.D.S. • POVERTY • RAMPANT CRIME

MASS STARVATION • NUCLEAR THREAT • TERRORISM

Is there a solution?

In answer to our urgent need...

THE CHRIST IS IN THE WORLD

A great World Teacher for people of every religion and no religion.

A practical man with solutions to our problems.

He loves ALL humanity.

WHAT IS HE SAYING?

*"The problems of mankind are real but solvable. The solution lies within your grasp.
Take your brother's need as the measure for your action
and solve the problems of the world."*

*"The answers to your problems are simple indeed... without Sharing and Justice, man will know no peace.
Trust in Sharing to relieve the agony of the world."*

*"Allow Me to show you the way forward into a simpler life where no man lacks;
where no two days are alike; where the Joy of Brotherhood manifests through all men."*

WHEN WILL WE SEE HIM?

*"It is My intention to reveal Myself at the earliest possible moment,
and to come before the world as your Friend and Teacher."*

*"When you see and hear Me you will realize that you have known for long the Truths which I utter.
Sharing and Justice, Brotherhood and Freedom are not new concepts.
From the dawn of time mankind has linked his aspiration to these beckoning stars.
Now, my Friends, we shall anchor them in the world."*

"Christis here, my Friends. Your Brother walks among you."

•

For information
TARA CENTER, P.O. BOX 6001, N. HOLLYWOOD, CA 91603 USA

FULL PAGE Ad appeared in USA TODAY

19

HEADING FOR A GLOBAL CRISIS

THE NEW AGE BLUEPRINT FOR CONTROL

**Preparing
The World
For An
Imitation
Christ**

The New Age Movement leaders, in recent years, have been testing the waters to see if an imitation Christ is acceptable to the world.

Millions in the United States are already into transcendental meditation [TM], yoga, mind control and other Eastern cult mysticisms. Famous motion picture and singing stars have made pilgrimages to India to "worship" at the feet of the "Master."

They and countless others like them are ripe for a strong delusion. Satan's plan is to <u>imitate</u> the prophesied return of Jesus Christ.

Lola Davis, a New Age writer, states that the New Age "Christ" is " . . . the One for whom all religions wait, called <u>Lord Maitreya</u> by some in the East, Krishna, Messiah, Bodhisattva, Christ, Imman Mahdi."

She states that this "Christ" will " . . . bring new revelations and further guidance for establishing the World Religion."

Where does this New Age Christ live?

Davis explains that the New Age Christ resides

on a different plane of consciousness from that which we experience. There he directs the Masters,

> a group of advanced souls, most of them discarnate [without human body] . . . known variously as the White Brotherhood, The Great White Lodge, the Masters of Wisdom, the Hierarchy and the Angels around the Throne.[7]

Creating A New Global Society

Further in this book, Davis states that this group of "advanced souls" is directed by Lord Maitreya in the East and Christ in the West. The Plan is to create a new global society that will welcome a World Religion for the New Age.

What are they waiting for? A global crisis! Alice Bailey, head of the Lucis Trust, has written several books which detail The Plan. She states that this New Age "Christ" will make his grand entrance when a global crisis arises. At that time " . . . Christianity will be eclipsed by the new religion."

Where will be the headquarters of this New Age leader? Jerusalem! This "Christ," they say will promise that there will be no third world war. He will make his entrance as a messenger of peace. And he will convince the world that he is "The Christ" by his ability to do miracles. Is it any wonder he is the great imitator!

Who are these New Age followers and where do they come from?

---

[7]Lola A. Davis, *Toward a World Religion For The New Age* (Farmingdale, N.Y.: Coleman Publishing, 1983, p. 186).

**Ready
To Take Over
In A New
Global
Crisis!**

In the first chapter of her book, *The Aquarian Conspiracy*, Marilyn Ferguson writes:

> *The Aquarian Conspirators range across all levels of income and education, from the humblest to the highest.*
>
> *There are schoolteachers and office workers, famous scientists, government officials and lawmakers, artists and millionaires, taxi drivers and celebrities, leaders in medicine, education, law, psychology. . . .*
>
> *There are legions of conspirators. They are in corporations universities and hospitals, on the faculties of public schools, in factories and doctors' offices, in state and federal agencies, on city councils and the White House staff. . . .*[8]

The followers of this New Age "Christ" are already being indoctrinated into the New Order. They are just waiting for a **global crisis** to strike so they can usher in their "Messiah." The Plan is for this New Age leader to proceed to Jerusalem and stand on the Mt. of Olives. Can you see how Satan is the great imitator!

LUCIFER IS THEIR GOD

David Spangler, a New Age writer, in his book, *Reflections of the Christ*, states that:

> *Lucifer comes to give us the final . . . Luciferic initiation . . . It is an invitation into the New Age.*

---

[8]Marilyn Ferguson, *The Aquarian Conspiracy*, (Los Angeles, Calif., J. P. Tarcher, Inc., 1980, pages 23, 24).

Mithraism Teaches That God and Satan Will Be Reconciled

He further writes:

> *Christ is the same force as Lucifer . . . Lucifer prepares man for the experience of Christhood . . . Lucifer works within each of us to bring us to wholeness as we move into the New Age.*

This theme of merging Lucifer with Light and wholeness originated in Babylon and in Persia. It was the cult of <u>Mithraism</u>. The theme of this cult was that Satan and God would be reconciled. Mithraism taught reincarnation and the progression of the soul through stages. This is what the New Age Movement teaches today.

New Agers are big on their brand of meditation. Over 14 Million Americans have taken meditation courses. The New Agers believe that through meditation man can become a god!

In recent years the old practice of spiritualism has regained favor among New Agers. They call it <u>Channeling</u>. Channeling is the process by which a person calls up a demon spirit to communicate with him. New Agers believe these spirits are all–knowing and possess the knowledge of the Mystery of the Ages. They now strive to harness their satanic power in a Global Mind-Link that will establish the New Age Kingdom!

20

CREATING THE MASTER RACE

THE QUEST FOR NEW AGE GODHOOD

"Ye Shall Be As Gods"

New Agers believe that modern man is evolving into a race of gods. They have fallen for the ages old lie that Satan told Adam and Eve in the garden: "Ye shall be as gods."

One popular New Age writer, a Moslem mystic wrote:

> There is only one question.
>
> And once you know the answer to that question
>
> there are no more to ask . . .
>
> Who am I?
>
> And to that question
>
> there is only one answer . . .
>
> I am God!

What are New Agers striving for? A master race, a super intelligence and human immortality. They hope to achieve this by the year 2100.

New Agers are looking for an "evolutionary leap" to occur instantaneously that will project them into a superhuman higher consciousness. Then, they say, they will become a god. And at last "enlightened" man will rule the universe!

ANTICHRIST . . .
A Persuasive Orator

What better way to stir a nation to action overnight! By way of prime time television he will plead:

Give me your mandate to get government back on its feet again. Give me the power to restore the working class to dignity . . . to smash the selfish few who control the billion-dollar multinational businesses and whose only allegiance is to the making of more profits . . . at your expense.

Let me put back nourishing food on your table so your child won't have to live on the edge of starvation!

Let me put back dignity into your home . . . so your husband does not have to beg for meager wages!

Let me put a roof over your head . . . that is a home and not a hovel! And one that you can pay off in a reasonable amount of time with a reasonable interest!

Let me put a future into your life so you can see your sons and daughters live in a land of the free and the brave!

I cannot do this if I must struggle through a government that is overgrown with weeds that strangle the very breath of progress . . . a government that feeds only its self-interests . . . and a 3 Million work force of federal employees who are leeching the very lifeblood of your happiness and future security!

I can only do this if you entrust me with ABSOLUTE POWER!

Give me this MANDATE and I will exercise this power as your faithful steward . . . slashing and cutting out the cancer of corruption so once again you can be proud . . . very proud that you are an AMERICAN!

Can you imagine what the results would be with such a stirring speech? As Hitler filled the void for a dying Germany . . . so Antichrist will be able to fill the void for Europe or United States on the brink of chaos!

THE THEOLOGY OF TWO ROOT RACES

New Agers Believe That The Problems Of The World Are Created By Christians!

New Agers promote the theory of <u>two</u> root races:

1. **God–status** [the superior root race]. See themselves as <u>positive</u> thinkers. Some New Agers refer to this as the "Yogic Kingdom of Heaven on earth." They believe that two–thirds of humanity will advance into the New Age Kingdom.

2. **Lower Consciousness** [inferior root race]. Referred to as <u>negative</u> thinkers. These are Christians and Jews who refuse to deny a personal Jehovah.

New Agers believe the problems of the world are caused by Christians. They reason that if Cosmic Consciousness . . . unity, peace and love . . . is to be ushered in Christians must first be disposed of. Since Christians, they say, are <u>negative</u> forces, a super–human race of man–gods, led by a New Age "Christ" cannot evolve until these <u>negative</u> forces are removed.

New Agers do not believe in individual salvation. Their theology calls for <u>collective transformation</u>. Maharishi Mahesh Yogi, founder of Transcendental Meditation [TM] states:

> *There has not been and there will not be a place for the unfit . . . In the Age of Enlightenment there is no place for ignorant people.*[9]

---

[9]Maharishi Mahesh Yogi, *Inauguration of the Dawn of the Age of Enlightenment* (Fairfield, Iowa: Maharishi International University Press, 1975) p.47.

**They Seek
A
Global Crisis!**

To solve their problems New Agers are looking for a global crisis, a World War 3, to eradicate Christians from the earth. [One can see how the Rapture would certainly be welcomed by them as an efficient "Christian disposal system."]

Of course, New Agers do not believe in the Rapture. They believe that Christians . . . "will have passed into spirit to <u>rethink</u> their attitudes."

Christians in this spirit world, they say, will be reeducated and rehabilitated and given a chance to change their minds. If they do change their minds, they can then become eligible to return to this world.

In the minds of many New Agers . . . Christians are the concentrated evil that is Antichrist. They are this evil because they deny the divinity of man. New Agers do not believe in the Battle of Armageddon as a war fought with weapons. Rather, they say it is a battle of <u>consciousness</u> . . . the <u>superior</u> root race vs. the <u>inferior</u> root race.

One New Age writer states that when man achieves god status man will be able to:

1. Turn off the sun and turn it back on again.
2. Freeze oceans into ice.
3. Turn air into gold.
4. Fly without wings.
5. Love without pain.
6. Cure by simply a thought or a smile.
7. Make the earth go backwards.

With this thinking in the Tribulation Period with Antichrist in control . . . one can see how the wholesale massacre of Christians will be justified as a humanitarian act to rid the world of negative forces and usher in "cosmic harmony and peace."

A NEW DAY . . . A STRONG DELUSION

**New Agers
Will Welcome
The Rapture!**

With the sudden disappearance of millions of Christians at the Rapture, the New Agers will take this as an affirmation of their doctrine. It would not be surprising if Antichrist would declare an international holiday!

Those who remain on earth . . . and whose loved ones have been raptured . . . will believe the lie told them by New Age leaders. They will be told that negative forces have been "released" to a spirit world where they will be "shepherded into all truth" and then returned to take their rightful place in society.

Why would they believe such a lie? One reason may be because New Age leaders are already making plans for a New Age **Bible!**

Our Lord tells us:

> *All Scripture is given by inspiration of God, and is profitable for doctrine, for reproof, for correction, for instruction in righteousness.*

> [2 Timothy 3:16]

On the other hand, a New Age leader writes:

> *We can take all the Scriptures and all the teachings and all the tablets and all the laws . . . and have a jolly good bonfire . . . because that is all they are worth.*

The New Age Bible will have a New Age Christ and his 12–person Spiritual Cabinet. It will contain the teachings of various mystics, Rosicrucians, Buddhist and Hindu philosophies. It will encourage man to believe he is a god!

BACK TO EDEN

New Agers Have Nine Doctrinal Cornerstones

In their own way, New Agers seek to go back to the Garden of Eden to create their perfect world, without interference from God. The Bible tells us that in the Last Days, men would fall for seducing spirits and doctrines of devils. We see this happening today!

The New Age Movement has 9 doctrinal cornerstones:

1. Eastern mysticism
2. Mind control through psychology
3. Mystery cosmic teachings
4. The worship of science as revelation
5. Instantaneous evolution
6. Hedonism [self–indulgent pursuit of pleasure which says that no act is sinful]
7. Pantheism [God is not a person. Everything is God! All laws, forces, and manifestations of the self–existing universe are God]
8. Selfism [Secular Humanism]
9. Leadership by spiritually superior beings [Man is an evolving god who is governed by Satan and his demons who are superior and are angels of light]

SOMEWHERE OVER THE RAINBOW

Trojan Horse Theology

The New Age Movement is a master of Trojan Horse theology. They are coming out with their own Bible, their own god and their own 12 apostles. They already use the Rainbow symbol to signal their building of the Rainbow Bridge [antahkarana]. This is their bridge between the personality [man] and the soul [Lucifer] . . . their link with godhood!

21

TOWARDS A NEW WORLD ORDER

**THE COUNTDOWN
HAS ALREADY BEGUN!**

**Seeking
To Get
Clergymen
On Their Side**

The ultimate plan of the New Age Movement is to win as many ministers and laymen to their cause and to take over every Christian church! To start their plan the New Age Movement sponsored a worldwide event they called **The Harmonic Convergence**. This was held worldwide August 16–17, 1987.

On December 31, 1987, the New Age Movement followed this up with an even bigger media event. This event was called **GLOBAL MIND LINK**.

This event had far greater implications. Leaders marshalled up to 1 Billion of their New Age believers to <u>simultaneously</u> meditate and visualize the New Age's sinister and subtle aims. The purpose of the **GLOBAL MIND LINK** was to call on their spirit guides and "The Force" to initiate world peace and establish a New Age Kingdom on Earth led by the New Age "Christ." ["The Force" is Lucifer.]

The New Age Plan is very clear. It is to establish a One World Government and One World

**Building
A Global
MIND LINK!**

Religion headed by a reincarnated man–god known as the New Age Messiah or "Christ." That is why up to 1 Billion people in more than 100 countries united in a **GLOBAL MIND LINK!** This is Bible prophecy coming alive right now.

If you have my Salem Kirban REFERENCE BIBLE . . . turn to page 263 at the end of the Bible in the Revelation section. In Revelation 17:12,13:

> *And the ten horns which thou sawest are ten kings [10 world leaders] which have received no kingdom as yet; but receive power as kings one hour with the beast.*
>
> *These have **one mind,** and shall give their power and strength unto the beast [Antichrist].*

**Ready To Give
Power To
Antichrist**

New Agers are worshiping together with **one
mind** . . . to give their power to Antichrist! They
seek to unite all religions as one . . . to unite all
nations as one. To achieve this they first want
to undermine belief in Jesus Christ and at the
same time discredit the Bible.

The purpose of their media–event gatherings is
to tell the world that

    1. Man is divine.

They regularly call on their "spirit guides"

    2. To reveal to them whom they should serve
       as "The Christ."

These gatherings also serve as a concentrated
mind link as they call on the New Age "Christ"
to come forth to seize his kingdom and unite
all the world's religions **and** economies into
One.

**How The
Money
Manipulators
Work!**

One only had to watch television in the October,
1987 stock market crash to see how the fate of
the United States was mercilessly at the hands
of the manipulations of the London, Frankfurt
and Tokyo stock markets. The international
bankers had a field day. And a majority of them
are New Age leaders!

In some instances New Agers even chant **"666"**
in hopes of energizing their evil activities!

It is not surprising to learn that thousands of
church leaders have included their churches as
part of this fast growing New Age movement.
One New Age leader said that with the aid of
computers and telecommunications:

We are almost at the completion stage of bringing together all of the thousands of New Age groups, organizations and churches.

It's time for Christians to wake up from their slumber and get busy for Christ . . . **now**!

Most Americans Fall For The Lie!

Here is what some New Age Leaders believe:

Zbigniew Brezinski (Jimmy Carter's National Security Officer and organizer of the Trilateral Commission) believes that a one–world religion must be the basis of a **New World Order**!

Mortimer J. Adler (Aspen Institute) argues that Christianity . . . not the arms buildup, is the greatest threat to world peace!

Barbara Marx Hubbard (A 1984 Democratic VP nominee) it is alleged, claims that Christians must be "eliminated" for the sake of World Peace!

It is estimated that almost 70% of Americans now accept some or all of New Age teachings.

In fact, New Age/Occult training is now required for employees of most of the nation's major corporations and even government agencies including the U.S. Navy!

Some say the New Age groups are simply a strange mix of spirituality and superstition. This is a smokescreen definition. Actually the New Age is a carefully goal–oriented <u>Movement</u> which seeks a One World religious and economic unity headed by their self–appointed "Christ."

In the United States alone, there are over 2500 New Age <u>bookstores</u>! Many radio stations are now playing New Age <u>music</u>! And there has been a dramatic increase in New Age <u>magazines</u>! Even some millionaires have their own private gurus [Hindu spiritual advisors] who make house calls! Even the U.S. Army is exploring ESP!

SHIRLEY MACLAINE . . .
NEW AGE PROMOTER

"We Are All GODS"

In the ballroom of the New York Hilton hotel, some 1200 followers paid $300 each to have Shirley MacLaine teach them the New Age theology.

With crystal chimes in the background . . . MacLaine taught her new followers how to meditate on the body's various energy points [called chakras].

One person in the audience says, "With all due respect, I don't think you are a god."

Shirley MacLaine replies, "If you don't see me as God . . . it's because you don't see yourself as God."

MacLaine is coming out very well financially in her New Age venture. She has written 5 books which have sold over 8 million copies.

The New York Hilton meditation session was the first of a 15–city national tour to spread the New Age gospel. It is estimated she will earn over $1.5 Million from this tour alone! She also plans to open a 300–acre retreat in Baca, Colorado where customers can get weeklong meditation therapy. MacLaine said, regarding this retreat:

> *I want this to be all mine, my energy, my control.*
>
> *I want a big dome–covered meditation center and a series of dome–covered meeting rooms because spiritual energy goes in spirals.*
>
> *I want to turn a profit with this . . . so I can build another center and another. I want to prove that spirituality is profitable.*

NEW AGERS
PROMOTE STRANGE THEOLOGY

**Blending
All Religions
Into
ONE!**

The New Age Movement tries to blend into **one** the teachings of Hinduism, Buddhism, and other "isms" including a dab of sorcery and pantheism [the belief that everyone is God].

New Agers even say that Jesus spent 18 years in India learning the teachings of Hinduism and Buddhism.

New Agers seek a shortcut to happiness and use artifacts and relics as sacred objects to achieve this end. This has become big business and New Age followers buy:

> Tibetan bells
> Solar energizers
> Colored candles
> Crystals
> Quartz
> Onyx

plus New Age magazines, books and recordings.

**Their
Own Brand Of
Second Coming**

On a meadow on California's Mount Shasta, a New Zealander sells his New Age theology to a group of about 200. For $10 each, he tells them he speaks with the voice of Soli [an "off–planet being"]. A voice emerges which says:

> You are here to search for yourself. The highest recognition you can make is that I am what I am. All that is, is. You are God. You are, each and every one part of the Second Coming.

Others, too, are profiting from New Age theology!

EX–HOUSEWIFE . . .
A PROFITABLE PROPHET

**Speaking
Through a
35,000 Year–Old
Warrior**

A channeler is one supposedly through whom another speaks. In the tiny town of Yelm, Washington, a housewife claims that a 35,000-year–old warrior named Ramtha . . . speaks through her.

Her name is J.Z. Knight. She says Ramtha once lived on Atlantis [a legendary island supposedly to have existed near Gibraltar and to have sunk].

Here is a sample of Ramtha's "wisdom":

> Who be I? I am a notorious entity.
>
> What I am here to do is not to change people's minds, only to engage them and allow the wonderments for those that desire them to come to pass.
>
> I have been you, and I have become the other side of what you are.

J.Z. Knight has performed for thousands of people. Her charge: $150 per session! These fees have enabled her to live in a luxurious mansion complete with spa and swimming pool and Arabian horses. She has a staff of 14.

Hear
Gabriel
For $15

Another channeler charges $15 a customer for supposedly channeling the archangel Gabriel. Since New Agers believe in reincarnation . . . this channeler says she was married to St. Peter and after "Peter was crucified . . . I was thrown to the lions after being raped."

A New York Wall Street Lawyer runs a $1.7 million center with 3000 students a month learning various aspects of Zen practice, Kung Fu and Astrology.

BATTLE LINES ALREADY DRAWN

Introducing
20 Million
To
Reincarnation

When Shirley MacLaine's television mini–series, "Out on a Limb" was shown . . . some 20 Million Americans were introduced to basic New Age teachings including **ESP** . . . Mind over Matter . . . reincarnation and telepathic communications. We were told that we are GODS. This is the same lie that Satan told Eve in the Garden of Eden.

In Christian homes we have children who watch cartoons like **"She–Ra"** and **"He–Man"** and television shows like **"Highway to Heaven," "Starman,"** and **"The Wizard"** which open up ideas of mysticism, occultism and eastern religions.

**Infiltrated
Into
Government,
Business, and
Education**

The New Age Movement is not just another cult. It is a powerful coalition of <u>thousands</u> of <u>groups</u> and powerful leaders . . . in government . . . in media . . . in education and in business!

Do you know the problem with a majority of American Christians. We're so busily engaged in self–indulgence that we could care less about people worldwide dying without Christ!

The most popular Christian <u>radio</u> programs are those that deal with psychology, marriage problems and raising children . . . when all those answers are found in the Word of God [if people would only read it]!

The most popular religious <u>television</u> shows are those that offer healing, prosperity and those that are engaged in "monument" building to have the BIGGEST ministry!

And while we divert all our energies to a plastic Christianity, the New Age Movement presses on with a singular goal of ushering in their "Christ."

The Coming
ONE WORLD CURRENCY!

Trilateralists and financial power brokers are swiftly moving to a One-World currency!

Their goal . . . to make countries surrender their national sovereignty over their _money_ systems. When this occurs, these same countries will ultimately surrender their _political_ sovereignty!

We are witnessing the beginning of the climate that will eventually usher in ANTICHRIST!

PART FOUR

22

HOW YOUR CASH WILL BE CONTROLLED!

TRILATERALIST GOAL
OF A ONE–WORLD CURRENCY

Surrendering National Sovereignty

Trilateralists supported by powerful international banking interests have designs on your money. Their goal is to create a One–World currency. And they are rapidly achieving that goal!

Their first goal is to make countries surrender national sovereignty over their <u>money</u> systems. When this occurs, [and it will], these countries will ultimately surrender their <u>political</u> control!

We are witnessing the beginning of the climate that will eventually usher in **<u>Antichrist</u>**!

Major nations around the world . . . including Communist countries . . . have <u>already</u> introduced <u>newly designed</u> currency to their citizens. France, England, Belgium, West Germany plus Iron Curtain countries have jumped on the bandwagon! Even the United States has been planning the introduction of this new money for years. They will not make drastic changes initially . . . but subtly change the currency in a two or three phase program.

YOUR NAME IS SURE TO BE IN ONE OF THESE COMPUTERS!

The United States Government knows you by a number. And federal agencies are turning to computers . . . which, at the touch of a button . . . can produce instant information on millions of Americans. Here are some major examples:

SOCIAL SECURITY ADMINISTRATION
Your Social Security number will soon become a universal number.

INTERNAL REVENUE SERVICE
Computer tapes store details from tax returns of over 75 million citizens. These tapes are made available to the 50 States.

U.S. SECRET SERVICE
About 50,000 persons are on computer who might tend to harm or embarrass the President or other high Government officials.

F.B.I.
Fingerprint files of over 86 million people now on computer.

DEPARTMENT OF AGRICULTURE
Keeps data on over 850,000 people.

DEPARTMENT OF TRANSPORTATION
Almost 2.7 million citizens who have been denied driver's licenses are on computer.

PENTAGON
Maintains files on some 7 million military personnel and civilians who have been subjected to *"security, loyalty, criminal, and other type investigations."*

VETERANS ADMINISTRATION
Keeps files on 13.5 million veterans and dependents.

DEPARTMENT OF LABOR
Has computer files on 2 million persons in federally financed work . . . all coded by their Social Security numbers.

DEPARTMENT OF JUSTICE
Computer bank has names of more than 14,000 individuals who have been involved in riots and civil disorders since mid–1968.

DEPARTMENT OF HOUSING AND URBAN DEVELOPMENT
Maintains records on 4.5 million who have bought F.H.A. homes.

With this federal computer network, there is virtually no limit to the volume of information that can be made available at a moment's notice on just about every American.

A MAJOR PROPAGANDA DRIVE

**Creating
A Reason
For A
New Money
System!**

The first major step was to convince Americans of the need for new money. And, on the surface, their explanation seems reasonable. We were told that the new money system was designed to stop the counterfeiting of American money. Yet what most people do not realize is that 80% to 85% of all counterfeiters are caught before they even pass a single counterfeit bill!

Look at this: Of the more than $25 Million in counterfeit money actually passed in the last year, only a few million was good enough to fool bank tellers. In today's Trillion dollar economy . . . a few Million is hardly enough to get excited about as an excuse to change the entire currency.

What is the underlying reason for the sudden switch to new money by major governments? The planners of a WORLD GOVERNMENT are speeding up plans towards a GLOBAL SOCIETY! Their goal is to establish a One World Government by the year 2000!

THE DAY NEW MONEY BRINGS NEW RESTRICTIONS

**Your
Rights
Will Gradually
Disappear!**

You could wake up one day and find the use of your money restricted by law. You may discover when you go to the bank . . . you will only be able to withdraw 5% or 10% of your savings within any 3 month period. In the Tribulation

Period an identifying number will be required on one's hand or forehead. A laser light will read both the hand and the new currency! Of the 3100 savings and loans, 500 are already bankrupt. This will be one more reason to restrict withdrawals of any sizeable amount of cash!

Entering
A New Era
Of Control

Canada was first in this hemisphere to come out with the New Money. It announced that the money was needed to counteract counterfeiters . . . yet virtually no counterfeiting takes place in Canada. The new Canadian currency has a special strip embedded in it. When a new Canadian bill is placed in a unique currency reading machine . . . it announces the denomination of the bill inserted . . . in an electronic voice in both French and English!

NEW TECHNOLOGY FRIGHTENING!

There is technology now present [with this new electronic strip on each bill] to:

1. Keep a record where that $10 or $100 bill has been traveling in the last 60 days or more. Such transactions reports would be of value to IRS and other government agencies.

2. When you cross state borders or go abroad, a computerized "money machine" could read exactly how much currency you are carrying in your wallet or pocket . . . without you revealing it [or even being aware that a machine is exposing your financial privacy].

If the IRS or any other government agency wanted to do it, the technology is already available to develop a satellite spy device so accurate it could beam right into your home! The electronic strip in your money may make this possible!

The Marking System is already here. In the Tribulation Period...in order to buy or sell...each individual must wear an identifying Mark either on their hand or forehead. Here is an artist's conception of how this event may occur. These illustrations are from a book by **Salem Kirban** titled **666 PICTORIAL**. If you wish this book, send $5 to SECOND COMING, Inc., Box 278, Montrose, Pa. 18801.

23

THE COMING CURRENCY SWITCH

**THE ULTIMATE GOAL:
DEVALUATION OF THE DOLLAR?**

**The
First Step**

One day in July, 1983 a market survey was conducted in a Buena Park, California shopping mall. People were shown various colors and designs of what was termed "new U.S. dollar bills." The Patterson Organization in Cincinnati, Ohio was the first to report this consumer survey.

It was later discovered that a consumer research firm from Illinois had been hired by the Department of Treasury Bureau of Engraving to determine the public reaction to various types of new money designs.

Three variations of U.S. currency were shown. The new bills were shown in various colors. The Federal Reserve seals were replaced by a reflective rainbow and some designs incorporated holograms. [Holograms give a three dimensional effect and change colors as they move back and forth.]

It was learned that in the past 10–12 years an <u>international</u> committee had been formed. Its purpose: to coordinate currency changes among member governments!

TOWARDS
A ONE–WORLD MONEY SYSTEM

**The
Coming
One World
Currency**

In June, 1989, Alan Greenspan met with the Senate Banking Securities Subcommittee. Greenspan is the chairman of the Federal Reserve.

Senator Jim Sasser (D–TN) asked him:

> *The overriding theme of today's hearing is the <u>globalization</u> of capital markets. Now national boundaries, we've learned, have very little meaning in today's economic development . . . it appears to me that costs of borrowing ought to be approximately the same, if in fact we are one worldwide capital market, and why isn't it?*

Greenspan, in effect, remarked that when each country can create its own currency . . . problems arise and there is no uniformity between nations. He suggested that this could be solved if you fixed exchange rates . . . which is the equivalent of <u>creating a single currency</u>!

Since U.S. currency is not backed up by Gold . . . but simply in your confidence in the paper dollar . . . chaos can easily be triggered. Gold backing acted as a brake on inflation. Greenspan, in suggesting a central World Bank idea [without the stability of Gold] would create a <u>globalized inflation</u>.

CASH IN CIRCULATION ERRATIC

M–1 is the U.S. Treasury indicator that measures how much <u>cash</u> is in circulation plus

By the end of 1923, the dollar exchange rate was 2.27 U.S. <u>cents</u> for **one billion** German Marks! The Mark depreciated hourly.

German housewives in 1923 found it cheaper to burn worthless marks than to spend them. An inflationary spiral is again threatening many nations. Another such disaster could pave the way for Antichrist!

<u>checkable deposits</u>. In June, 1989, the M–l indicator fell by **$20 BILLION!** It had never dropped this much since even before 1959! This was an indication that businesses were pulling back and people were hoarding their cash. Thus the introduction of a new currency will flush out the old currency.

STEPS TO A WORLD BANK

A
Three Phase
Plan

The introduction of new U.S. currency is just the first step towards the United States joining the Common Market nations. Here's what may happen.

First   The U.S. will introduce **Phase 1** of the new currency. It will have some minor changes . . . an identifying strip running vertically on the bills. The U.S. says it will allow the old money to continue to be used for two or three years. But I would not count on this happening. The old currency could be considered worthless within one year or less. Those who have hoarded thousands of dollars will suddenly have to declare this cash and suffer a potential loss. [One way around this is junk silver and gold coins . . . which we will discuss later.]

Second After Americans have become familiar with the new money system . . . **Phase 2** will be introduced. This new

U.S. currency will have a mysterious "blank space" on the face of each bill. This will just be another step towards eventually conforming to a central World Bank!

Finally Because of runaway inflation and an unmanageable debt . . . the United States will eventually join the Common Market nations. It will be the only way out! It will accept a unified money system and will pave the way for the climate that will eventually usher in Antichrist!

Note that this is a step by step change that is <u>so gradual</u> that Americans will not realize they are being led down a path where eventually they will lose their sovereignty and national rights! When will this occur? My guess is by the year 2015.

NATIONAL DEBT <u>DOUBLING</u> EVERY 24 MONTHS!

**National
Debt
Out Of
Control!**

It is very difficult to secure the accumulated debt figure . . . that is, the debt the United States owes to other nations. It is very revealing to note that as recently as 1984 the United States was solvent in regard to other nations. [As an example, in 1983, the U.S. had a surplus of $89 Billion.]

But suddenly we began the downward plunge. Below is the accumulated debt the U.S. owes to other nations. It is staggering!

1986	**$267 Billion**
1987	**$378 Billion**
1988	**$532 Billion**
1991	**$1 Trillion**

**What's
A
Few Trillion
Among
Friends!**

Now take the 1988 figure of a debt of $532 Billion. The **interest** we will have to pay on this debt is estimated at <u>**$53 Billion**</u> [a little over 1 Billion a <u>week</u>]!

To compound this problem . . . financial advisor, Lawrence Patterson reports:

> *These interest payments will be <u>reinvested</u> in other assets upon which <u>still more interest</u> will have to be paid . . . and on and on and on . . . <u>until the $ is inflated to 0 value</u>.*

The above is our **foreign** debt. Our **federal** debt will soon surpass $4 Trillion Dollars. One industrialist has recently written a book on economics in which he projects that by the year 2000, the U.S. federal debt will climb to $13 Trillion Dollars!

Many predict that paper currency will eventually be abandoned as we enter a cashless society! World banks are already working to this end!

WOULD THE DOLLAR BE DEVALUED?

**Devaluing
The Dollar!**

Every financial consultant is aware of the growing and troublesome U.S. trade deficit. What better way to stop this landslide than to issue new currency . . . massively devalue the dollar . . . so that it costs more to buy overseas goods.

**Tragic
Consequences**

As Lawrence T. Patterson points out:

*A new Mercedes car instead of costing $65,000
. . . might cost $150,000.*

*A Nikon camera from Japan instead of costing
$295 . . . might end up costing $995.*

*In other words . . . imports would cost 3 to 4
times the current amount in U.S. dollars.*

Patterson goes on to say that Treasury securities may be the <u>worst possible place to keep your savings under such currency manipulation</u>.

NUMBER OF MISSIONARIES DECREASING

We have already witnessed how the dropping of value of the U.S. dollar has made it difficult for U.S. missionaries to stay on the field. As an example, about 10 years ago a missionary could live on support of $400 a month in Japan. Today, that same missionary can hardly exist on $4000 a month!

This is a subtle way of closing down mission fields around the world. And this would certainly make the humanists, the international financiers and the New Age supporters happy!

24

CURRENCY RECALL MAY BE SWIFT AND SURPRISE!

**NEW BILL FURTHER CURBS
FINANCIAL FREEDOM**

**Phase One
Now In
Operation**

Initially, the Bureau of Printing and Engraving was going to have a fine metallic strip run through the currency. It was later decided to have a clear, polyester strip woven into the paper and run vertically on the left side of the Federal Reserve seal. Printing will appear on the length of the narrow strip.

Bill Baxter, in his Baxter Economic Newsletter, revealed that the Government is emptying its vaults of the old money and stopping printing of old bills. Some of the uncirculated old bills now surfacing date back to 1969!

Baxter states:

> Government spokesmen will insist to the very last moment that no recall is planned. But this is the practice of all governments. They cannot announce in advance that a currency is going to be recalled or devalued. It would create havoc in the financial markets. Such announcements are usually without warning and when financial markets are closed.

WORLDWIDE MONEY CARD

On New Year's Day, 1981, Greece became the European Community's tenth member. These Common Market nations, totaling some 280 million people, have now become the world's number One economic and trading power.

How long will it be before we see a unified Worldwide Money Card used not only by the 10-nation federation but also by the United States? It could occur within the next 10 years!

 This is the symbol for EUROPA (Europe) UNITED. It now appears on automobiles and on bank credit cards throughout Europe.

U.S. Master computer terminals may be at two loca-
Luxemburg tions: the United States and Luxemburg. Luxemburg, at present, is a Common Market nation but in the future it may serve as Master Computer Headquarters. It now houses the EEC (European Economic Community) Computer commonly called ***"the Beast!"*** The two blocks will identify which Master Computer should register the transaction.

 This single chip microprocessor will have your entire life history on it. It will identify your food purchasing restrictions, whether you are a Christian, your address, those in your family unit, personality traits, your bank withdrawal limitations plus a host of other data. It will contain 10,000 transistors . . . yet be no bigger than the grid shown to the left. This grid, not any larger than a dime, will determine whether you can buy or sell!

a66687 This series of vertical lines in two blocks plus a
000287771b number and letter code will identify your <u>voice print</u> and will be used to activate "clearance access" at the supermarket check-out counter.

Face Scan You will have your photograph taken by a <u>Face Scan</u> camera. This likeness will appear on your Money Card and a Laser Beam will scan your computer photo to verify your identification.

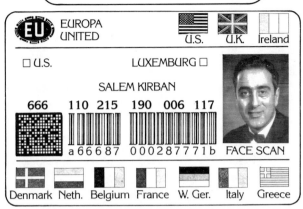

Universal Numbering System

EUROPA UNITED — EU

U.S. · U.K. · Ireland

☐ U.S.   LUXEMBURG ☐

SALEM KIRBAN

666   110 215   190 006 117

a 6 6 6 8 7   0 0 0 2 8 7 7 7 1 b   FACE SCAN

Denmark · Neth. · Belgium · France · W. Ger. · Italy · Greece

*Here is what your Money Card **may** look like!*

Besides the various identification cross-match systems described on the page to the left, there may be a universal numbering system. One possible number format is pictured above. Note that it is a series of <u>three</u> sixes **(6+6+6).**

Here is what these universal numbers could represent:

666   This may be the International World Code to activate the Master Computer at central headquarters.

110   This may be the National Code to activate the Super Computer at the United States base station.

215   This would be your phone number Area Code.

190   This would be your Zip Code region number.

006   This would be your Zip Code for the town or city in which you live.

117   This would be your <u>individual identifying number</u> which, in effect, is your personal Zip Code number.

The identification number . . . **666** . . . now appears already on Computers shipped to Israel. It also appears on shirt labels from China, shoes from Italy, floor tile made in the U.S. as well as some Government forms. Strangely enough, the prefix **666** is also used by some department stores in their billing invoices to the customer!

Dr. Mary Stewart Relfe, author of <u>When Your Money Fails</u>, offers some interesting applications on how the number **666** is now in wide use around the world.

U.S. Dollar Has No Backing Except Your Confidence

Baxter continues:

> *The Roosevelt Administration made everyone turn in their gold in the 1930's. After the people had done so, the Government jacked up the price, pulling off one of the most baldfaced robberies of its citizenry since the colonies were settled.*

> *Then in the 1960's, the Government said that all silver certificates that were convertible into silver bullion had to be turned in. Until 1971, foreign countries could exchange dollars they were holding for U.S. gold. The U.S. backed down on that promise too when President Nixon closed the gold window.*

WILL THERE BE A BANK HOLIDAY?

It Can Happen Here!

In June, 1985, Raul Alfonsin, President of Argentina, declared a national bank holiday. He then announced that the new currency would replace the old peso on a <u>one</u> new peso for <u>1000</u> old peso basis!

In March, 1986, Brazilian President Sarney declared a four–day bank holiday and created a new currency! Long lines of people, anxious to make withdrawals, were seen at the 24–hour cash machines.

It is doubtful whether the U.S. would declare a bank holiday. This would create chaos. But they will not allow the old currency to stay in circulation very long. They may give a two–week or one month grace period.

WILL $100 BILLS BE RECALLED?

**Tightening
The Noose
Of
Control**

The Reagan–Bush administration have encouraged bills in Congress that would grant less financial freedom. Under the Omnibus Drug Initiative Act (HR 5210) some unlimited powers are given.

Ron Paul, in his Investment Letter, states:

> *The U.S. government has long wanted to eliminate $100 bills, to hinder the present use of cash, and to pave the way for the cashless society. As a high Fed official told me, this is still objective #1 at the central bank. But because of all the publicity, and the Fed's success in labeling anyone using $100s as a drug dealer, the unofficial economy has often switched to $50s.*

Ron Paul sees the possibility of a recall of both $50 and $100 bills. Paul feels that drug dealers will have inside information on the recall date. And those who really will be hurt will be innocent middle class Americans. Paul believes that banks will be instructed to turn over the name and Social Security number of everyone who brings in more than $3000 in $50s and $100s. And even though you paid taxes on this cash . . . you would be entered into the IRS, the Treasury and Justice Department computers. Now, can you see how the Mark of the Beast emerges in the Tribulation Period!

Ron Paul suggests that those with $50 and $100 bills on hand should start converting them over to the less conspicuous $20 bill.

THE CURRENCY TRANSACTION REPORT

**The Plan Few
People Even
Know Exists!**

CTR (Currency Transaction Report) is a report banks file that require your name, address, occupation, Social Security number and amount of cash involved. In the past this Report was only required when a transaction of $10,000 or more was made. This is now being lowered to $3000. However, this bill really wipes out all ceilings for requiring a CTR report. It could be lowered to $1000 or even $500. But there is even more latitude in power given to the Omnibus Drug Initiative Act.

Banks could also be ordered to determine what you are going to use the money for and when . . . according to Ron Paul.[10] This will generate more paperwork. But this would give an excuse for the Treasury and Federal Reserve to use the international computer network known as **SWIFT.**

S	ociety for
W	orldwide
I	nterbank
F	inancial
T	elecommunications

In 1 year Americans already fill out approximately 2.5 million Currency Transaction Reports which banks must process and send to the Treasury within 15 days!

---

[10]Should you wish to subscribe to Ron Paul's Investment Letter, write to 1120 NASA Boulevard, Suite 104, Houston, Texas 77058 for information.

**Freedoms
Slipping
Away**

In 1978, President Jimmy Carter introduced the Right to Financial Privacy Act. This was to protect customers of financial institutions from unwarranted government intrusion into their financial records.

In 1986, Congress (upon request from the Reagan administration) amended this law. The amendment requires any bank to hand over financial information about any customer <u>without</u> his permission. It also holds the bank harmless from any legal liability. It will be interesting to see whether George Bush's "kinder and gentler nation" includes a further stripping away of individual privacy.

25

NEW WORLD CURRENCIES PAVE WAY FOR ANTICHRIST!

**NEW MONEY
HAS UNEXPLAINED BLANK SPACE**

**Towards
A
Unified
Currency**

There is an international drive to unite all currencies under one central authority. In October, 1987, the **AMUE** [Association for the Monetary Union of Europe] met secretly to discuss this objective.

Here is what they recommended:

1. The European Currency Unit **(ecu)** should replace existing national currencies.

2. All European central banks should combine into one European Central Bank **(ECB)**

3. These Banks should then issue **ecu's** as the official unified currency.

4. Government leaders, international bankers and corporations should then promote a one world currency issued by a world central bank!

American Express is now offering ecu–denominated credit cards. Anyone who knows Bible prophecy can plainly see the handwriting on the wall!

FINANCIERS
PLAN TO CRUSH SMALL BANKS

**90% of
U.S. Wealth
Owned By
60
Families**

We have already witnessed savings and loans being squeezed out of the financial market. The next step will be to squeeze out small banks so that control is in the hands of the few. Many are unaware, as an example, that 90% of the wealth in the United States is owned by only 60 families!

In 1985 officials from the Morgan Bank in New York met with officials from the Trilateralist French Bank, Credit Lyonnais. They decided that in order to get world cooperation for a unified currency they would have to create a new association. This they did. They call it **ECUBA** [European Currency Unit Banking Association].

Prominent bankers from Europe, Japan and the United States are using the **ECUBA** to their advantage. And now the **ECUBA** has created an offshoot organization they call **BFEC** [Banking Federation of the European Community]. The first priority of the **BFEC** is to shut down the small banks, develop a conglomerate of a few huge banks . . . all united under one Central Bank. Thus a World Central Bank!

The automatic scanner pictured above automatically reads the Universal Product Code. As the product is passed over the plate, a laser beam shines <u>in all directions</u> through the **X** opening.

What the customer cannot see is the warning label that appears <u>underneath</u> this **X** plate. Various machines read either: ***DIRECT LASER RADIATION*** or ***DO NOT LOOK AT LIGHT...IT MAY BE HAZARDOUS TO YOUR HEALTH!*** Years from now, we may learn it causes cancer...who knows! Perhaps Antichrist will use this technology to limit food purchases only to those who have the Mark!

THE COMING WORLD CENTRAL BANK

**Three
Central Banks
To Control
Currency**

The Plan is that by 1996 there will be <u>three</u> central banks that will control the currency and world economy. Those three banks will be:

1. The Federal Reserve Bank [the dollar]
2. The European Central Bank [the ecu]
3. The Central Bank of Japan [the yen]

The next step after this will be to <u>merge</u> all three banks into <u>one world central bank</u>. Then they will issue a single world currency! It would appear that the **IMF** [<u>I</u>nternational <u>M</u>onetary <u>F</u>und] will become the World Central Bank!

THAT MYSTERIOUS BLANK SPACE

**Towards
A Unified
Currency**

If you examine any of the new currency designs issued by foreign countries [including Communist countries] they all have one thing in common . . . an unexplained **blank space**!

These blank spaces are not accidental. They have been planned that way by international bankers! This is Step One towards a unified one world currency.

This blank space is for a Central World bank <u>overprint</u>. This all–powerful bank may be the **IMF** [International Monetary Fund]. And the new one world currency may be called the **Phoenix**!

In light of this, some financial analysts suggest:

1.   Get out of debt as soon as possible.

NEW WORLD CURRENCIES
PAVE THE WAY FOR ANTICHRIST!

Pictured below are the new currencies of four major European countries. Eac
of these Trilateral-controlled nations have designed currency which incorpora
ONE COMMON FEATURE! All these bills provide about the same amount
BLANK SPACE!

Pictured on the <u>left</u> is the new currency of SCOTLAND. On the above <u>right</u>
the new money of BULGARIA. Even nations that were once communi
countries are leaving a blank space on their new money! Is this not the fir
step towards a *world currency denomination* that will pave the way f
Antichrist!

2.   Put your numismatic gold coins in a safe place . . . not bank safe deposit boxes.

3.   Check with your financial advisor on when to sell bullion coins and gold stock.

4.   Don't build up a supply of old dollars. [They will become worthless once the new currency is introduced]

5.   Pray

Leaders Seek A New World Order!

Even the Soviets, first under Mikhail Gorbachev and now under Boris Yeltsin, are seeking a world government ". . . to guarantee peace and the future of mankind."

Is the new money system, with its standardized blank space on all the currency, the <u>first step</u> towards that One World system?

Time will tell! But, right before our very eyes, we are witnessing the countdown that will eventually trigger the Rapture and then the tragic 7–year Tribulation Period. Are you ready?

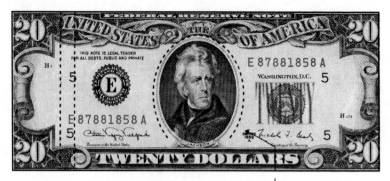

⌐ **Translucent polyester filament**   └**Microscopic type**

26

THE NEW MONEY IS HERE!

Major Change
Insures
Control

The first major change in U.S. paper currency <u>since 1929</u> was introduced in 1991. Pictured above is a sample of what the New Money looks like. The new bills contain a polyester filament running vertically on the left hand side. This filament is translucent. This means it will let light pass but diffusing it so that objects on the other side cannot be clearly distinguished.

The filament is imprinted with an extremely small lettering running from top to bottom. The lettering identifies the bill. A $100 bill reads USA 100, a $20 bill reads USA 20, etc. These identifying marks are only able to be read if held up to direct light. This thread cannot be copied by copiers since they use reflected light . . . not translucent light!

▶ **HAVE YOU NOTICED** lately how your currency looks shabby, worn out and faded? The reason fresh old style currency was not introduced to replace it was so that this New Money could take over. In August of 1991, local banks began

Heading Towards A New World Order!

to receive $50 and $100 bills with the translucent polyester filament and microscopic type. This was followed later by $20s, $10s and $5s.

▶ THE REASON GIVEN THE PUBLIC for the introduction of this New Money is to catch the counterfeiters. Last year alone some $66 Million in counterfeit money was seized. But many government officials secretly confess, according to reports, that the counterfeiting of money is an insignificant problem. When you consider the Billions the Government spends . . . $66 Million is a drop in the bucket. [Remember, it takes <u>1000 Million</u> just to make <u>$1 BILLION</u>!]

According to the McAlvany Intelligence Advisor [July, 1991], about 62% of the total value of U.S. currency in circulation is held in $50 and $100 bills. Don McAlvany reports that:

> *The real reason for the currency call–in will be to drive hundreds of billions in cash out of the underground economy and back into the banks where it can be counted, recorded, reported to the IRS [if the amount is over $1000], and taxed [or re–taxed] if the owner cannot prove he paid taxes on it.*

One U.S. Treasury official would like an <u>overnight exchange of old currency</u> to the New Money system to catch people by surprise. However, at this time . . . the initial change in currency was gradual over several months.

▶ WHAT WILL HAPPEN IS that merchants will be reluctant to accept the old $100, $50, $20, $10 and $5 bills . . . fearing they may be counterfeit. Eventually it will be almost impossible to get rid of old currency without taking it to a bank. And at the bank <u>you will have to fill out an IRS form</u>! If you think you can just take your old money to the bank now and exchange it a little at a time . . . <u>you may be in for a surprise</u>! This will not work! Bank tellers have already been notified to keep track of individuals who bring in small amounts of cash over a period of time. **Those who do will be reported to the IRS.** Don McAlvany reports many banks will no longer accept cash in amounts over $3000. Therefore, most of Old Money will never be re-deemed. The result — a massive windfall profit for the government.

Using The Technique Of Gradualism!

▶ THE INITIAL CHANGES IN THE NEW MONEY will, to most people, appear insignificant. <u>And that's exactly what the financiers want you to think</u>. Slowly, but surely, more changes will occur over the next few years. Some of the changes may be the introduction of <u>bar coding</u>, chemical coatings that could trigger electronic sniffers.

<u>Holograms</u> [3–dimensional pictures] could be used and other hightech devices that will make it easier for the Government to track down currency.

In fact, the day will come [if it is not already here] when from outer space . . . a signal could be beamed on a man walking down a street in [as an example] Iowa Falls, Iowa and reveal how much money he has in his pocket . . . what his name is . . . and where he lives!

**Watch Out
For
Step No. 2**

GRADUALISM–A progressive action taking place step–by–step, little–by–little, continuous and imperceptible. <u>Imperceptible</u> means un-noticeable, undetectable.

Remember the story of the frog put into a kettle of cold water on the stove. He swam happily along. Gradually and imperceptibly the water got warmer and warmer. As it did the frog continued to swim and was lulled to sleep. When the water started to boil . . . it was too late. The frog had suffered the consequences of **GRADUALISM.** <u>That's exactly what is happening here in the U.S. today</u>. The changes in this **NEW MONEY** will be <u>imperceptible</u> changes. Perhaps one day, <u>overnight</u>, drastic changes will occur. Each bill will be a different color. A mysterious blank space will appear on the currency. And you will have to change to the new currency within 72 hours. <u>Many financial analysts believe that day will come</u>!

On January 22, 1991, Gorbachev withdrew all 50 and 100 ruble notes from circulation . . . declaring they would be invalid at midnight! Citizens were given 3 days to exchange their notes. <u>However only 250 of their rubles could be exchanged</u>. All bank accounts were <u>frozen</u> and no more than 500 rubles a month could be withdrawn. **AND LOOK AT THIS:** By the Soviet Government invalidating [making worthless] 50 and 100 rubles notes . . . which is 1/3rd of total Soviet currency . . . the Soviet Union realized a $96 Billion robbery of Soviet citizens savings!

Below are suggestions by many financial analysts on how you can protect your assets in this rapidly changing economy!

WHAT CAN YOU DO
TO PROTECT YOUR ASSETS?

**Cash To Give Way
To
Computers
And
Credit Cards**

If you are afraid of banks, Savings and Loans and insurance companies . . . many financial analysts recommend:

[1] Do not hold more than $1000 in cash as your cash may be suspect in time of a currency call–in.

[2] Hold a large portion of your liquid assets in U.S. Gold and Silver coins. Some recommend $20 gold double eagles or Morgan or Peace Silver Dollars. Don McAlvaney suggests silver dollars that trade over 15% of bullion content. He says these are extremely liquid and far more private than bullion coins.

[3] Minimize use of credit cards. Avoid using debit cards or "smart" cards.

[4] Minimize the use of your Social Security Card. Use it only when you have to on tax forms, in opening bank and securities accounts etc.

▶ FINANCIAL ANALYSTS REVEAL that <u>all monetary instruments</u> such as money orders, cashier's checks, bank drafts and travelers checks will carry identifiable coding <u>to reveal the name of the individual using them</u>. The reason: to track

**Enter
The
Cashle$$
Society**

down the use of cash! Already the U.S. Post Office has introduced their new Money Order. One analyst reports that ". . . all individuals who hold large amounts of cash . . . will soon find it impossible to exchange their old currency for the soon–to–be–released new currency." <u>They recommend converting $50 and $100 bills to $20s, $10s, and $5s</u>.

▶ WE ARE ENTERING THE AGE of the Cashless Society and the Age of Antichrist where we will be controlled by a numbering system and computers. The future will witness

[1] New Cash Reporting Requirements

[2] The Computerization of the American People

[3] Your Privacy Being Invaded and

[4] The Day Your Dollar Dies!

If you would like to learn more of God's plan for tomorrow, these books by Salem Kirban may be of interest to you:

On Antichrist and the Tribulation

Countdown to Rapture	$7.95
The Rise of Antichrist	7.95
Satan's Angels Exposed	7.95
Satan's Mark Exposed	7.95
666 Pictorial	6.95
666/1000	8.95

On the Millennium

666/1000	$8.95

On Heaven and Hell

What Is Hell Like?	$3.00
What Is Heaven Like?	$3.00

Order from your local bookstore. If they cannot supply you, you may order direct from: Salem Kirban, Box 278, Montrose, PA 18801 U.S.A.

Add $2 for shipping.